# Investigative Forensic Hypnosis

# INVESTIGATIVE FORENSIC HYPNOSIS

By
JOE NIEHAUS

CRC Press
Taylor & Francis Group
Boca Raton London New York

CRC Press is an imprint of the
Taylor & Francis Group, an **informa** business

*Photography by Darin Preston.*

CRC Press
Taylor & Francis Group
6000 Broken Sound Parkway NW, Suite 300
Boca Raton, FL 33487-2742



ISBN 13: 978-0-8493-8133-1 (hbk)



**Visit the Taylor & Francis Web site at**
**http://www.taylorandfrancis.com**

**and the CRC Press Web site at**
**http://www.crcpress.com**

Library of Congress Card Number 98-22629

**Library of Congress Cataloging-in-Publication Data**

Niehaus, Joe.
Investigative forensic hypnosis / by Joe Niehaus.
p. cm.
Includes bibliographical references and index.
ISBN 0-8493-8133-9 (alk. paper)
1. Forensic hypnotism. 2. Forensic hypnotism — United States.
I. Title.
HV8073.5.N54 1998
363.25'4—dc21

98-22629
CIP

# *Foreword*

Most people are fascinated with the magic and mystique associated with hypnosis. That such an "entertainment" vehicle, however, would be called upon for serious purposes, especially when it comes to law enforcement, tends to heighten one's skepticism. What are the results when someone suggests forensic hypnosis as a tool to help solve a crime? Is this comparable to involving a psychic or the likes of David Copperfield to unravel a case?

During my 27 years of experience in law enforcement, I have seen the practical applications of hypnosis. Sgt. Niehaus used hypnosis to help solve a hit-and-run accident when the victim was able to remember a description of the car. There was also an incident when a witness to a burglary saw a suspicious vehicle but was unsure of specifics about it. Through hypnosis, he was able to describe, in detail, the vehicle and writing on it, as well as the driver.

This book presents the practical applications and the scientific side of forensic hypnosis. It explains forensic hypnosis in a simple-to-understand way, and it legitimizes something that many may think of as "parlor trickery".

This all-encompassing guide discusses forensic hypnosis from its most basic definition through to its practical use in the courtroom. Eliminating the mysticism of forensic hypnosis may be impossible, but I am certain that this text will provoke thought and perhaps shed a light of acceptance on doubters. Many common questions I have had about forensic hypnosis have been answered, not only through texts such as this but also through my own experience as witness and observer.

**Jim O'Dell**
*Police Chief*
*Kettering, Ohio*

The need for and use of investigative forensic hypnosis in the criminal justice system are ever increasing. Joe Niehaus, who has been a street patrol officer and investigator and is presently a supervisor for the Kettering, Ohio, Police Department, has a firsthand awareness of this extremely vital tool. Mr. Niehaus, who co-wrote *Hypnosis Unveiled,* has written this book to help meet the continuing challenge faced by those who use hypnosis. His outstanding law enforcement background and his valued expertise in hypnosis qualify him to author this most important and informative handbook, which covers topics ranging from the origin of hypnosis to its uses today.

Mr. Niehaus has divided the discussion on hypnosis into two parts: The Essence of Hypnosis and Investigative Forensic Hypnosis. The primary focus of this handbook, however, is on the latter topic. Mr. Niehaus explores this subject in detail, relating how hypnosis is used as a tool to help a witness go back in time to recall what he has seen. In the area of law enforcement, this ability is of great importance, because it allows investigators to determine additional facts regarding the cases they are investigating, whether criminal or civil.

Mr. Niehaus cautions, however, that using hypnosis as an investigative tool for law enforcement must be done correctly. In this regard, Mr. Niehaus has outlined specific guidelines and procedures required.

Today, hypnosis is an accepted tool in law enforcement. Its use and success continue to grow. My special thanks are extended to Joe Niehaus for his work in hypnosis. His enthusiasm, work, and dedication are a credit not only to himself but to all of law enforcement.

**James M. Connell**
*Assistant Prosecuting Attorney*
*Montgomery County Prosecuting Attorney's Office*
*Dayton, Ohio*

I would like to thank Joe Niehaus for his interest in and concern for ethical hypnosis. As a student at the Ohio Peace Officers Training Academy, Joe attended one of the first classes in forensic hypnosis, where he recognized the usefulness of and need for forensic hypnosis as an additional tool for investigations. Through his thirst for learning and research, he has led the way in promoting the ethics and proper uses of hypnosis in the courtroom. This book clearly identifies the uses and strategies suitable for the most novice investigator. In this day and age, we need any and all help there is in completing our investigations.

**Nell R. Orndorf, M.A.**
*International Executive Director*
*Association to Advance Ethical Hypnosis (AAEH)*

# *Preface*

It was in the early spring of 1984 that I first encountered forensic hypnosis. It was my first year in the criminal investigation unit of the Kettering Police Department in Ohio. I attended a one-day seminar held at the University of Cincinnati on forensic hypnosis, but I, like many in class that day, was quite skeptical of how hypnosis could help law enforcement. I had seen how hypnosis was portrayed on television, in movies, in stage shows, by magicians, and even in novels. What I could not figure out was how getting people to act strangely or say things to make people laugh was going to help me or my department solve criminal cases. To me, hypnosis was part of the entertainment world or was performed by frauds trying to fleece money out of their marks. Then the instructor explained and demonstrated the power of the human mind, and from that point on I gained a new respect for this "parlor trick".

What the instructor showed me that day was that hypnosis is capable of giving the police and prosecution a method to enhance one of the most powerful assets available when putting cases together — a good witness. Hypnosis allows witnesses to go back and review what they saw and to extract the most minute details that had previously been forgotten due to the excitement of the moment or fear. Numbers on license plates can suddenly be unscrambled, or digits that were missing previously can now be filled in. The interior of a car can be described by a witness, and small dents and scratches can now be described. All this and more can come out of a successful hypnosis session. That day I also learned that hypnosis is a tool, and like many tools it has a number of different applications. Stage shows, magicians, and entertainment are just some; witness memory enhancement is another.

Hypnosis first appeared in our court system in 1958 in the case of Cornell v. Superior Court of San Diego, 52 Cal. 2nd 99. The irony of this first application of hypnosis in a criminal proceeding was that it was put to use not by law enforcement but by the defense. The case centered around the murder of Maria Martin and the accused, Paul Le Clair Conrey. The body of Maria Martin was found near a cemetery with her dress pulled up. There were scratches on her body, her underwear was a short distance away, her shoes were still on her feet, and her hair was up in curlers. There was a broken cocktail glass about 5 feet away from her body, which was lying in a shallow ditch. Tire tracks showed that her body had been driven over by a car, which then left the area.

The investigation led right to Paul Le Clair Conrey. When his vehicle was found, the tires were compared with the impressions made at the crime scene, and a positive identification was made. Further forensic evidence showed fragments of Martin's skull were on the underside of Conrey's vehicle, and hair matching Martin's was found in the interior of the car, as well as curlers similar to the ones still in Martin's hair.

The detectives on the case interrogated Conrey, who could remember events fairly well up to 11:00 in the evening, but then, because he had been drinking heavily, his memory failed. He could remember that he had been in several bars during the night drinking with friends. After that, all he could remember was waking up in his car, parked the wrong way on a one-way street. The detectives discovered witnesses who could place Conrey at a bar with Martin, which was the last time she was seen alive, and Conrey was arrested.

Attorney Richard Cornell was Conrey's legal representative. Being faced with his client's alcoholic amnesia, Cornell knew he had to do something to retrieve Conrey's memory of what happened after 11:00 p.m., and the only way he knew to do that was with hypnosis. Cornell knew a hypnotist by the name of Richard N. Mikesell, and after consulting with him on the case, he decided that hypnosis could help with Conrey's memory.

There was a problem, however. The prosecutor and sheriff of the facility in which Conrey was housed would not allow hypnosis to be used on Conrey, and they certainly would not allow information gained in such a way to be entered into court. Cornell took his plea for hypnosis to the Supreme Court of the State of California. During the hearing, the prosecution claimed that they had nothing against hypnosis, but because it was so unusual it should not be allowed in a criminal trial. Justice J. Peters replied that just because something is unusual does not mean it has no value, and he allowed the hypnosis session to take place.

Mikesell conducted his session with Conrey and pieced the events of the night together. Conrey had been drinking with his friends at various bars and ended up at the one where Martin was. He was trying to get another woman to leave with him and have sex, but all she wanted to do was to talk and drink. Martin then approached Conrey and told him that she would go with him. Conrey bought her a drink just to get her to leave him alone. Finally, Conrey gave up on the other woman and decided to leave. As he got to his car, Martin asked him if she could go with him and Conrey consented. He decided to drive her to a location he knew well as a child (the cemetery), where he planned on having sex with Martin, but he passed out. He awoke to find Martin yelling at him, and he told her to let him sleep. When he awoke again, Martin was not in the car with him, so he drove home.

Conrey's new information, when combined with the evidence, shed a whole new light on the case. Apparently, while Martin was in the car she removed several of her curlers, apparently to let her hair down for Conrey. Perhaps feeling the need to go to the bathroom, she exited the car and removed her underwear. She made her way to the bushes, but on her way back she fell and passed out. She fell directly in the path of Conrey's car, so when he awoke, still intoxicated, he did not see Martin and assumed she had left. He decided to drive home and in the process drove over Martin, killing her.

Cornell took this information into the courtroom and presented his information to the jury. The prosecution still got their conviction, but the charge was the lesser offense of manslaughter. Instead of the death penalty, Conrey received a sentence of 5 years to life and was eligible for parole after 1 year. At the end of the trial, Judge Mehedey, the trial judge, commended Cornell for his efforts and for saving Conrey from the gas chamber.

Since that time, hypnosis, unusual though it is, has been gradually accepted as a means for helping investigators find out what happened. The goal of this book is to familiarize the reader with hypnosis — not as a parlor trick, but as a successful and dependable investigative tool that assists in investigations. It does so not by magically solving crimes, but by providing clues and details with which the investigators can work.

The information presented within these pages is designed to assist the hypnotist who is performing investigative hypnosis, investigators of cases who are considering the use of hypnosis, prosecutors who will be involved in cases involving hypnosis, and judges who may have to determine if hypnosis has been applied appropriately.

This book is divided into two sections. The first is designed to explain hypnosis from a scientific approach. All the misconceptions are stripped away, and a logical approach to this unusual phenomenon is followed. You will learn what facts have been uncovered about hypnosis, and you will be able to separate truth from myth. The media's past barrage of misleading information will be set aside as you begin to understand how our minds and hypnosis work. Once you understand hypnosis, you will begin to see the potential for its use in law enforcement. You will see that we are still exploring its potential and that we have learned much since the trial of Conrey. You will also see that in regard to hypnosis, as is true for many other fields, there are those who will misrepresent it, but after reading this book, you will be able to clear up all of those misconceptions and determine when hypnosis will be of value to a particular case.

The second part of the book will guide you in investigative hypnosis. Armed with a clear understanding of hypnosis, you will be able to apply it to the criminal justice system. There are procedures that must be followed to ensure that the memory being retrieved belongs only to the witness and has not been suggested by the hypnotist. If you are wondering whether a witness' hypnosis-refreshed memory is acceptable in court, in the second part of this book you will learn the route hypnosis has taken through our court system, from the initial 1958 case to the Supreme Court's decision regarding Rock v. Arkansas. And, you will find that a witness' hypnosis-refreshed memory is, indeed, admissible, as long as proper procedures are followed.

The defense attorney will mount an all-out campaign to protect his client, and in cases involving hypnosis there will be controversy. The defense will present their own "hypnosis expert" to discuss the methods used during the hypnosis session in question. If you are the investigator, prosecutor, or hypnotist, you must be prepared to answer many questions involving hypnosis in general, not just forensic hypnosis. That is why this book takes a two-step approach. You must clearly understand the tool before you can put it to use. You need a firm foundation in hypnosis before you can ever use it to benefit a witness' memory or to assist in a criminal case.

In the fight against the criminal element, law enforcement must seek out every available advantage. The ability to improve the quality and amount of information obtained from victims and witnesses will always be an asset. Come along and discover how to harness the strength of hypnosis and use it against those who would harm our society and citizens.

# *The author*

**Joe Niehaus** earned his A.S. in Police Science and B.S. in Criminal Justice from the University of Cincinnati. He is currently a sergeant with the Kettering Police Department in Ohio and has been in law enforcement for 21 years, 9 of which were spent in the criminal investigation section. In 1984, he took his first class in forensic hypnosis and has been utilizing this tool for police agencies ever since. He is certified in forensic and clinical hypnosis by the Association to Advance Ethical Hypnosis and the International Society of Professional Hypnosis. He is a member of both agencies, and was an instructor at the Association to Advance Ethical Hypnosis conference in 1995.

Mr. Niehaus was a certified fraud examiner and a member of the International Society of Auto Theft Investigators, Southern Ohio Fraud Investigators, the National Association of Bunco Investigators, and the Ohio Auto Theft Investigators Association. He was awarded the Officer of the Year distinction by the Kettering Kiwanis in 1992.

An instructor at the Miami Township Police Academy and the Sinclair College Basic Police Academy in Ohio, Mr. Niehaus has also developed the Kettering Police Department's Defensive Tactics Program of Realistic Integrated Use of Force Training and was a speaker at the Association of Law Enforcement Trainers seminars held in 1997 and 1998. He has conducted seminars for local residents in street awareness and survival skills, as well as seminars for the Ohio National Guard and the Red Cross.

In 1990, his street crime awareness book, *The Sixth Sense: Practical Tips for Everyday Safety*, was published (Blue Bird Publishing). As a result, Mr. Niehaus appeared on CNN's *Daywatch* program and on several radio stations nationally. In 1994, he co-authored *Hypnosis Unveiled*. He has also served as technical advisor for Sharyn McCrumb, a popular mystery writer, and was a speaker at the Malice Domestic Writer's Conference in 1994. He has written articles appearing in *Law and Order Magazine, Police Marksman Magazine, Black Belt, Fighting Stars,* and local newspapers.

# Contents

# *Dedication*

This book is dedicated to the memory of Fran Renner.
Her ethics in hypnosis were beyond reproach,
and her enthusiasum unmatched.
She was my teacher, hypnotist,
and most of all my friend.
She will be missed.

*Part one*

# *The essence of hypnosis*

## chapter one

# A foundation of hypnosis

When one mentions the word "hypnosis", reactions vary, mostly because of a lack of understanding on the subject or a perception forged from stories, the media, and gossip. Before hypnosis can be applied to law enforcement there must be a thorough understanding of the subject, so that when being cross-examined on the witness stand the forensic hypnotist can testify with authority and knowledge, not relying upon myths, innuendo, and media hype. Keep in mind that a subject such as hypnosis can be a very hot topic at a trial, and the defense will utilize all of the myths to portray it as trickery or fabrication. Only a clear explanation and, if need be, a practical demonstration can show this police tool in its true light.

To begin with, the name "hypnosis" comes from the Greek *hypnos*, which means "sleep". It was so named because while a person is in hypnosis it appears they are sleeping. Their eyes are closed, their body is relaxed, and they respond slowly like a person just about to fall asleep or just waking. However, as the reader progresses through this book, you will soon see that the name "hypnosis" actually is one of the first myths that needs to be dispelled, because whatever hypnosis is, it is not sleep.

Down through the ages, hypnosis has been saddled with many images, most of which have been unfavorable except to those who have studied it or benefited from it. Even today, these same images persist, despite many scientific discoveries documenting the usefulness of this phenomenon. Visions may come to mind of people up on a stage, completely under the spell of the hypnotist and performing various acts to the delight of the audience. Old movies, such as *Dracula*, starring Bela Lugosi, in which he used the power of hypnosis to lure his victims away from safety and into his clutches, is typical of portrayals that have helped tarnish the image of hypnosis. These and other such media images have been passed from generation to generation, often by writers using hypnosis to further a plot or to enhance suspense, not by those who treat it in a professional or scientific manner. Facts that do not add anything to the story are often left out. These myths and stories have made it difficult to develop and use hypnosis to its fullest potential. Indeed, there is still much to be learned about the subject, because the study of the human mind is ongoing and continues to show us just what a magnificent machine it is.

Adding to the troubles for hypnosis is the fact that no one, including those who have worked with it for years, can say exactly what it is. Because it is not tangible, defining it in its totality is a problem. The effects of hypnosis can be explained easily enough, and the feelings of being hypnotized can be described, but when it comes to pinpointing exactly what hypnosis is, current definitions all seem to fall short.

It is actually easier to say what hypnosis is not, rather than what it is ... which brings us back to the first misconception, its name. Even though hypnosis is formed from a word meaning sleep and usually a person's eyes are closed during hypnosis, it is not a sleeping state. Sleep is the physical realm we enter when the external world is shut out, our conscious mind allows the subconscious to open up, and we experience a dream state. When we sleep, all of our focus is internal; unless there is a particular sound that wakes us from our slumber, we are able to shut out most external stimuli.

Conversely, in hypnosis, while a person enters a dream-like atmosphere, they are still aware of who and what are around them. Individuals in hypnosis can hear everything that is being said, know who is in the room, and are alert to sounds and odors. In fact, with the exception of their eyes being closed and their bodies being relaxed, hypnosis subjects are fully awake. This may surprise you and may perhaps be a little difficult to understand; however, during a hypnosis session there is no question as to what the hypnotist says. Also, not only does the sense of hearing work during hypnosis, but all of the other senses are operating, as well. Touch, smell, taste, and sight all work just as they did before a person entered the state of hypnosis. Sight is the only exception, in that hypnotists usually ask subjects to close their eyes and to keep them closed until they are asked to open them.

Perhaps a better way to understand hypnosis can be gained with the image of a chart numbered from 1 to 10, with the lowest number representing a person who is fully awake and alert (see Figure 1.1). The number 10 will then represent someone who is totally asleep. Take a moment and offer a guess of where you think hypnosis would fall on that scale. When I use this example in classes on the topic of hypnosis, the usual guesses tend to be at the higher end of the scale, with 7 and 8 being popular. Which did you pick?

The actual number may surprise you, because hypnosis falls between 3 and 5 on this scale. Hypnosis is not the unconscious state, nor is it the deep sleep often portrayed by various media. By looking at the chart, you can see that the hypnotic state is actually closer to one of being fully awake and alert than it is to being sleep. This scale is often met with some skepticism, but the following examples may help to demonstrate further that hypnosis is not sleep.

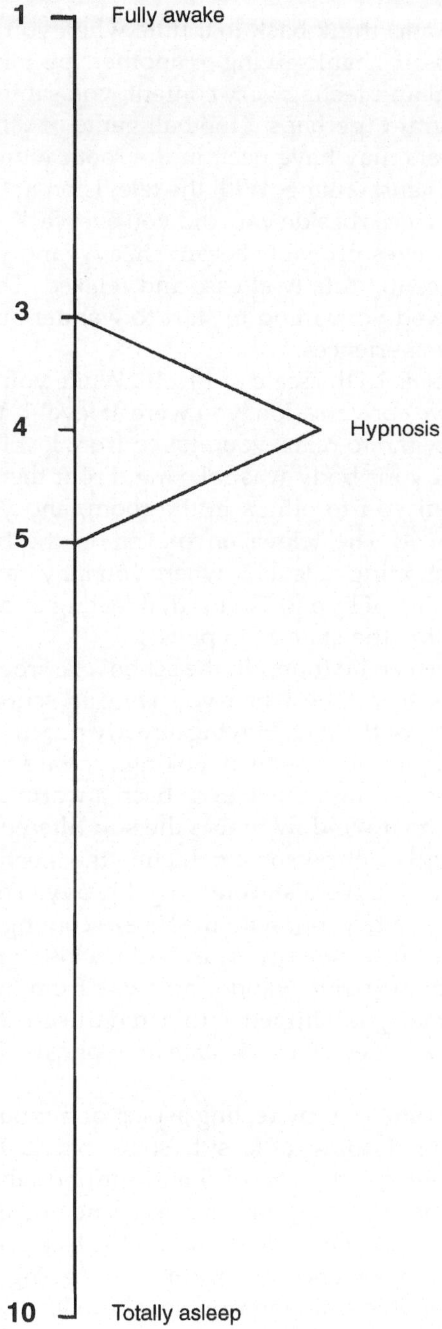


**Figure 1.1** Location of hypnosis on a scale from being fully awake to being totally asleep.

Take a moment and think back to a time when you had just finished a large dinner, perhaps at Thanksgiving or another special holiday time. Having finished the meal and feeling very content, you sat in front of the television to watch a program (perhaps a football game or other sporting event). Other family members may have been in the room with you, watching the game along with you and talking. With the television in front of you and the low hum of friendly voices beside you, did you ever feel yourself start to drift off to slumber? Your eyes probably became heavy, and you sank lower into the chair or couch, feeling totally at ease and relaxed. Then, at that point of relaxation, you allowed your mind to start to wander and to think of other times and pleasant experiences.

Now let's refer back to the scale of 1 to 10. While you were eating dinner and involved in active conversation, you were at level 1. When you sat in the chair or couch and began to relax, you moved from level 1 to 2, because you were still awake but your body was relaxing. From there, the conversation started to move from you to others in the room, and you were no longer actively involved in it. The television played in the background as you relaxed even more, slipping to level 3, where you may have even closed your eyes and entered a state of hypnosis. It is that feeling of being totally relaxed and comfortable that is the state of hypnosis.

Another example can be found in the school classroom or at a corporate meeting. Think back to a time when you were in school or in a meeting, perhaps in the middle of the day. Having already put in a hard morning and feeling tired, you might not have been looking forward to the subject matter about to be discussed. It might have even been a warm day, and you found yourself sitting next to a window where the sun filtered into the room and warmed you. The teacher or person conducting the meeting was talking, but you found that your eyes were starting to get heavy. You might have even fought the feeling for awhile, but with the breeze coming in the window and the warm sun on your face, your eyes just had to close for a moment. As you were sitting there you began to wander off away from the topic, thinking of another place or time; you slipped into a daydream. It is that feeling of daydreaming that really describes the state of hypnosis, located between 3 to 5 on the scale.

This brings us to another interesting aspect of hypnosis — it is a natural act we all are capable of doing, at least to some extent. The only exceptions to this are children under the age of 5 and individuals who are mentally impaired. A natural act, you may wonder? Yes, and you experience hypnosis at least twice each day ... once before you go to sleep and again before you wake. Referring to our scale once again, notice that going from a waking state to one of hypnosis involves moving from level 1 to levels 3 to 5; to go further to sleep, we move to level 10. Each night we pass from the waking state into the totally asleep state. To reach that state, our bodies relax, and we drift off, just as described in the examples of the Thanksgiving meal and the classroom. When we sleep, though, we move along the scale even further; instead of remaining in that daydream state, we move into slumber. Then, just before we wake up, we again come from that deep sleep state to a waking state, passing through levels 3 to 5, where hypnosis is found. Thus, hypnosis is a natural part of our lives and we are all capable of achieving that state.

Another example may help to illustrate how hypnosis occurs. Imagine for a moment that you are in bed and sound asleep. Suddenly, the stillness of the night is broken by your alarm clock going off. The sound of the alarm enters your dreams and draws you out. You wake up enough to reach out with your hand and turn off the alarm. As you lie there in bed, still sleepy, you may think to yourself, "Just 5 more minutes and I'll get up." You are aware of where you are, even what time it is, but you are totally relaxed and enjoying the comfort of your bed. You may begin to think of other things. These feelings of relaxation and comfort represent a state of hypnosis, at levels 3 to 5 on our scale. In hypnosis, you are aware of everything that is going on around you; however, because you are relaxed and comfortable, you choose not to acknowledge these outside stimuli, just as when you choose to turn off the alarm and remain in bed for a few minutes more.

This relaxed feeling — the key to hypnosis — is the primary reason why, in 1840, the English doctor, James Braid, coined the term "hypnosis" from the Greek *hypnos*. As Braid worked with his patients, however, and explored this thing he called hypnosis, he found that in fact hypnosis was not sleep, because the patient was aware of everything he said. Aside from being relaxed with their eyes closed, they were very much awake. When he finally concluded that hypnosis was not a sleeping state, it was too late to change the name, and hypnosis became the accepted name for this phenomena.

This did not stop Braid from trying to change the name, though. He soon discovered that when he performed hypnosis on some of his patients, a one-on-one relationship developed, in which the patient was able to focus in on a single point or to focus on a subject suggested by Braid. Because of this narrow focus, Braid tried to change the name to one of a more descriptive term — *monoideism*. Societies being what they are, the term hypnosis persisted, though, and Braid's monoideism slipped by the wayside.

From the beginning, hypnosis has been difficult to describe, but if you take away nothing else from this chapter, at least understand that hypnosis is *not* sleep. Should you become a forensic hypnotist and become familiar with the many aspects of hypnosis, you will find yourself attempting to describe this phenomenon to others who have not experienced it. The daydream examples mentioned above may be of assistance to you in this regard, but as you explore this topic you may find other occurrences in everyday life that will help to model this natural state.

The hypnotic trance depicted by various media has furthered the image of hypnosis as sleep. I am sure you can think of at least a couple of movies where a character is walking around in a deep trance, performing a task that later in the story he cannot recall doing. This image is often encouraged by the stage hypnotist, who wants the audience to believe that the volunteers on

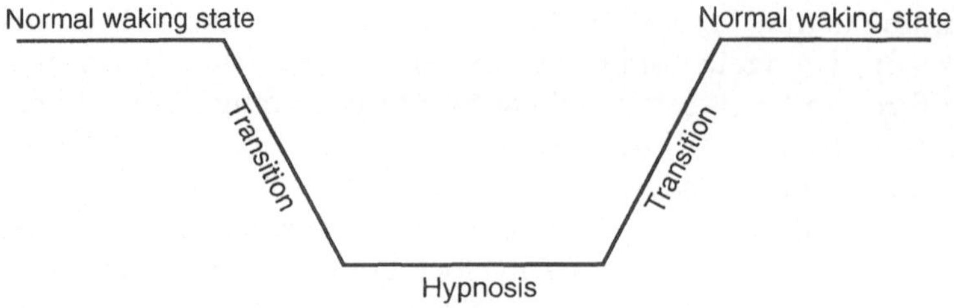


**Figure 1.2** Typical view of hypnosis.

stage are completely under his spell; however, this perception — that when people are hypnotized, they fall into a deep trance in which they have no control over their actions — is definitely *not* accurate.

Hypnosis is a fluid state that is constantly changing, just as a daydream is something that can come and go depending on what is happening around you. Look at Figure 1.2, which shows the way in which many people perceive how a hypnosis session occurs. The top line is a person who is awake and fully alert but then goes into the deep trance (demonstrated by the line traveling down) when hypnotized. The person in the hypnotic trance is represented by the line at the bottom of the chart. The person coming out of hypnosis and re-awakening is represented by the line drifting back up to the fully alert level.

Because hypnosis is neither sleep nor trance, Figure 1.2 is inaccurate. Contrast Figure 1.2 with the chart drawn in Figure 1.3. Again, the top line represents a person who is fully alert and awake. The line plummeting down represents a person entering hypnosis; the line resting on the bottom represents hypnosis. However, in this chart, you will notice that the person does not remain in hypnosis; rather, the line moves up and down in a wavelike pattern. That is because a person in hypnosis does not remain in such a state but floats in and out of this state.

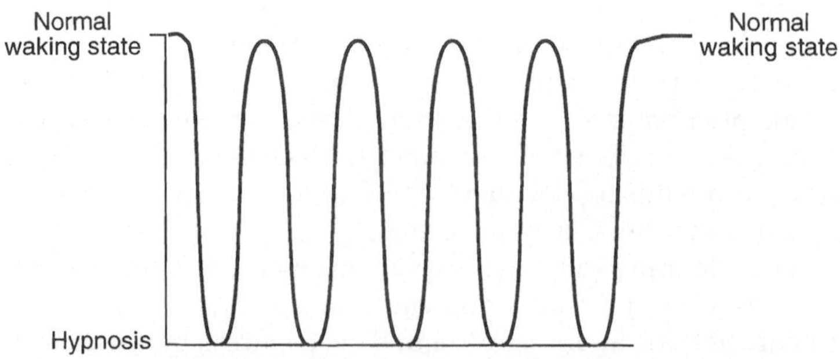


**Figure 1.3** Hypnosis actually is more like a wave than a straight line.

Many people, including me, who have gone into hypnosis often report afterwards that they did not feel as if they were in hypnosis because they heard everything that was being said, they were aware of what was going on in the room around them, and they were able to talk to themselves. Such feelings help to verify the accuracy of Figure 1.3. On a number of occasions, I have talked to myself while in hypnosis. I have even questioned whether or not I was hypnotized, but I kept my eyes closed in an attempt to assist the person hypnotizing me. However, even as I was convinced that I was not hypnotized, I was able to imagine the scene they were describing to me and found my arm floating upward at their suggestion, with my arm becoming lighter and lighter. Did I know my arm was drifting upward? Of course I did, but I allowed it to happen because I wanted to go along with the suggestion. So, I was in hypnosis and I was back out, only to return again and to come out again. This all happens very quickly, and it can almost seem as if there is no going in and out of hypnosis occurring.

The key thing to note here is that I allowed myself to go along with the hypnotist. This important point is often overlooked by those who portray hypnosis in an improper manner. The mind is a powerful tool, and we remain in control of it even in hypnosis. How can this be, you might ask? As you progress through this book you will come to understand that many of the stories about hypnosis are false (such as people being made to do absurd things against their will) and that the use of hypnosis on stage is more entertainment than an accurate portrayal of a useful tool.

This is a good opportunity to discover a little of this phenomenon yourself. At this point you will need a tape recorder or another person. Read the following passage into the tape recorder or hand the book to someone else to read it. Just relax during this brief exercise and allow the words to enter your thoughts. During the exercise, have your eyes closed, because this will enhance the effects, plus it has been shown that we live about 85% of our lives through our eyes. If we close them, there is a better chance for your experience to be more focused and detailed and thus much richer. When you are ready to begin this exercise, stand up and remain standing throughout. You (or the person you have chosen to read the words for you) should read the passage slowly, in a relaxed manner. The exercise will not be affected if you know the words beforehand; instead, it is your reaction to the exercise that will be of interest to you. (Begin speaking, or taping.)

> "With your eyes closed, take a deep breath and relax. Now raise your arms up directly in front of you. Have both palms facing down. Now turn the right palm up so that it is facing skyward. Very good. Relax. Clear your mind. Focus on my voice. I want you to imagine or visualize all the things I am now going to describe to you. I want you to imagine, just visualize me tying a string around your left wrist, the one with the palm

facing down. Attached to the other end of the string is a balloon ... a big balloon ... a large, helium-filled balloon, any color you'd like. When I let go of the string, you will feel a slight tug at the end of your wrist as all of the slack is taken out of the string. When I do this, you are going to feel the balloon carrying your arm up and up, and your arm will feel lighter and lighter. I let go of the string and you can see the balloon rise up as the string reaches all the way out and the slack is picked up. There is a pull on your wrist as the balloon now carries your arm higher and higher. You can feel it getting lighter and lighter as the balloon continues to drift upward and upward.

"Now focus your thoughts on your other hand, the one with the palm up. I'm going to place something in your hand. Something heavy, very heavy. Oh, you know what it is. It's that book. You know the one. The big book in the library. That dictionary that sits on the swivel stand. It has thousands of pages and it's heavy, very heavy. When I place this book in your hand, your arm is going to support all that weight but because it's so heavy your arm will begin to drift down. Think of all those pages, all that weight being held up by your arm alone. How tired that makes your arm, how heavy. I place the book in your hand and immediately you can begin to feel the weight and the strain it places your arm under. To relieve the strain, just let your arm drop lower and lower.

"Your other hand, however, keeps getting lighter and lighter as the balloon continues to drift upward towards the sky. Your arm feels so light and the string continues to pull it up and up and up. But your other hand has all that weight to support and it drifts down and down because it is so heavy.

"Now, hold your arms where they are and open your eyes. Once you have seen their position go ahead and lower both of them."

(End speaking, or taping.) Where were your arms at the end of this session? Many people find that their left hand drifted upward with the balloon and their right sank downward with the book. This shows how the mind can be influenced by suggestions. Was there really a balloon tied around your wrist? Of course not, but your mind allowed your arm to react as if there were. Was a book placed in your hand? No. Again, your mind allowed the image to influence the position of your arm. This little example also demonstrates the only ability a hypnotist has — the power of suggestion. Despite all those images portrayed down through the ages, a hypnotist can only suggest things to you. It is how you handle those words or suggestions that makes the difference.

This principle is demonstrated by the balloon-and-book example. Some individuals who undergo this same exercise find that neither hand moved in any direction; their hands and arms remained directly in front of them. The reason for this is that the suggestions made by the hypnotist were not accepted by them and therefore had no influence over them. They were able to resist the images described by counter-suggesting to themselves that they would not be affected by the words. This reveals the vulnerability of the hypnotist — that all hypnosis is self-hypnosis, and the ability to go into hypnosis depends upon the subject, not the hypnotist.

We have two minds — the conscious and the unconscious. Both are important for us to function, but each operates in a different manner. The conscious mind is that part of us that is with us all day long. It is that little voice in the back of our head that talks to us and tells us what is right and wrong. It is basically our conscious thoughts and acts, that part of our mind of which we are aware ... what is commonly referred to as your "mind".

The unconscious mind, though, is not as accessible to us. This part of our mind does not help us make decisions by discerning what is right or wrong or by "talking" to us. Rather, this part of the mind merely stores information just as a computer disk or large file drawer does. Everything that we have experienced in our lives is stored on this disk or in this file drawer. All sorts of details long since "forgotten" are actually still stored back there, in the unconscious part of your mind.

The reason we are not aware of the existence of all this information is that the conscious mind cannot handle being aware of such an immense volume of small, minute details and still function in society. Information that is no longer needed is put into a "file", and the conscious mind moves on. Just imagine for a moment what your mind would be like if you consciously thought of everything you have experienced since you were 5 years old. Your mind would be quite a jumble, with a whirlwind going on inside of your head. Your ability to focus on any given task would be extremely limited. So, in order for us to be able to function in society, only information thought to be of importance to the conscious mind is kept in our thoughts. Everything else is sent to the files.

This is very important because it is the information in those files that the forensic hypnotist is interested in. The smallest details of an incident are the very details that could help make or break a case. The only problem is how does one get to that information? One method, of course, is with hypnosis.

Looking at a photograph of ballpoint pens (Figure 1.4) will help illustrate how hypnosis allows us to access the information stored in the unconscious

**Figure 1.4** The pen with the cap on represents our waking state. The cap is our conscious mind, and the pen is our subconscious.

mind. For this example, let's say the cap of the pen is the conscious mind and the pen itself is the subconscious. When we are awake and fully alert, our mind is like the pen with the cap on. All experiences must go through the conscious mind, and we are only aware of what the conscious mind holds. If a person is being questioned by the police outside of hypnosis, this pen would be an illustration of how the mind is functioning. Only consciously recalled details will be given to the officer, because the subconscious mind has not been accessed.

When we use hypnosis, the mind operates in a different manner. During a hypnosis session, the conscious mind is asked (or given suggestions) to go on an imaginary journey. The conscious mind is directed to visualize something pleasant (as in the example earlier with the balloon and book). Such an imaginary journey is represented by the pen with the cap off. The conscious mind is awake and is aware of what is going on and what is being asked of it during hypnosis, but now the unconscious mind has opened up.

The unconscious mind is represented by the pen itself, and it rests alongside the cap because during hypnosis both minds are operating in their own way. When the suggestion is given to the conscious mind to go back in time, the subconscious mind goes right along and opens the file drawer for that particular year, month, day, or hour and retrieves all the information that has been stored there. In a sense, at this point, we have two minds both functioning, as the conscious mind accepts the suggestions of the hypnotist to go back into the past and the subconscious allows the stored images, emotions, and experiences to come forward.

This is not similar to a person having a flashback in movies or on television. In hypnosis, the stored information comes back in the form of memories just as if you are consciously remembering a special moment in your life. There are feelings associated with it, and different senses are involved. Details that we have long since forgotten are suddenly remembered, such as the name of a friend or a face or anything else we might have experienced.

When the mind is like a pen with a cap on it, it does not have the ability to call upon these stored memories as easily, because the conscious mind is the primary, active mind, while the subconscious holds all the stored information. But, when you think of the pen and cap sitting side by side as being representative of hypnosis, you can begin to see how both minds functioning and retrieving information reveal more information.

At this point we should address another issue regarding the state of hypnosis: A person cannot be "stuck" in hypnosis. During the session, the subject is able to hear everything that is said because the conscious mind is not turned off; it is merely being directed to a daydream. If there was an emergency of some kind, subjects would be able to open their eyes at any time and deal with the emergency, just as they would if they were awake and fully alert.

Remember back to the earlier discussion about when you might have been sitting in a classroom, you found yourself bored, and you started to drift off into a daydream. What happened when you were suddenly called on by that instructor? Most likely your eyes popped open and you found yourself fully awake looking around for a clue or two to help you answer the question posed to you.

The same thing would happen with hypnosis if someone were to enter the room and yell, "Fire!" The person in hypnosis would open his eyes, just as when a teacher calls a student's name. Taking this a step further, if a hypnotist were to give a subject a suggestion that the subject found offensive, the same thing would happen — the subject would open his eyes and confront the situation.

To explain this aspect of hypnosis to a class, I hold the pen in the hypnosis phase, with the cap and pen side by side. But, to demonstrate an unacceptable suggestion being offered, I return the cap to the pen, representing the same effect as a teacher calling a student's name. The conscious mind will not let you hurt yourself, so being presented with a suggestion you do not like would have the same effect as that found in the example of the book and balloon — the people who choose not to let their arms move do not accept the suggestion. Suggestions given must be acceptable to the conscious mind or they will have no effect.

Because of the many misconceptions about both hypnosis and the amount of control a hypnotist has over his subject, there are those who become interested in the subject hoping that it will give them an edge with the opposite sex by allowing them to impose their will. The truth is quite the opposite. In order for someone to go into hypnosis, three elements must be present. Without these three, it is impossible for someone to hypnotize someone else. These three are (1) freedom from fear, (2) willingness, and (3) confidence in the hypnotist. All three are equally important, and the lack of any one element will diminish any hope of the hypnosis session being a success. Let's take a moment and look at each one of these in a little more depth.

## *Freedom from fear*

In order for us to slip into a daydream-like state, our bodies must be in a relaxed state. In fact, relaxation is a very important to the success of hypnosis. Without relaxation, the body remains tense and guarded. See for yourself what being relaxed feels like. Take a moment to fill your lungs full of air. Let it out slowly, and then ease the tension out of your shoulders and body. Normally, when we are awake our bodies are tense, even though we may not be aware of it. The usual tension we experience as we function day to day, though, is much less than the tension present when we are afraid of something. Fear is a very powerful emotion.

Fear is able to reach deep inside of us and control us to the point that all we can focus on is the item we are afraid of. When a person is afraid, it is extremely difficult to relax, which seems common sense enough. Imagine for a moment the picture of someone totally relaxed and at ease. Maybe he is sitting in front of the fireplace in a large easy chair, sipping a glass of wine and just watching the flames dance around the logs — a nice, comfortable scene where you can imagine the person very easily slipping off to sleep. Now contrast that image with a person who is fearful. Think of how the face is pulled back, eyes wide open, mouth poised for a scream. Perhaps the person is in a room trapped by fire with no escape. Fear has gripped this person, and every muscle in his body is tense as he tries to figure a way out of the situation. A person in this situation certainly will not be able to relax; in fact, he is at the complete opposite end of the spectrum.

The same applies to hypnosis. If a person is afraid of hypnosis, for whatever reason, he will not relax. His fear will keep him from doing this. Take a moment to think about what you fear the most. What one thing would you not want to face? Now, just imagine yourself faced with that. Can you see yourself being able to relax in that situation? The same is true for people who are afraid of hypnosis. If they cannot relax, they will not go into a relaxed state, and they will not be able to create that daydream-like state necessary for hypnosis.

To overcome this, the hypnotist must take plenty of time to explain what hypnosis is so that, through education, the subject's fear can be conquered. Fear is a powerful emotion, though, and if the subject is still afraid of hypnosis no force on Earth can make them relax and go into hypnosis. Think about that for a moment. Can you be ordered into relaxation? Of course not. If you do not want to relax, there are no words I can say that will make you relax against your will. The hypnotist, then, cannot force someone to relax and cannot force a person into hypnosis, which leads us to the next element required for hypnosis.

## *Willingness*

To go into hypnosis, a person must want to; otherwise, they will not be able to. As we have discussed, no one can force anyone into hypnosis. In order to go into that daydream-like state, a person has to be relaxed. If a person does not want to do something and are forced to do it anyway, what kind of a mood will this person be in when performing that particular task? He will be tense and upset. Not exactly the picture of someone slipping into blissful slumber in front of a fireplace. Instead, when we resist a particular task, our defenses go up and we prepare for a confrontation.

To demonstrate this point in a classroom setting, I approach a person sitting in the front of the room and shake his hand, asking him his name. I may talk to the person for a moment or two before telling him that I want him to go to sleep and relax. Before he can answer, though, I yell at him to relax and continue to do this several times. By this point, the person is sitting back in the chair, eyes wide, and I know there is no way they are about to relax no matter what words I use.

The subject who is to be hypnotized is the only one who can control whether or not they will be hypnotized, which is good news for the hypnotist. Those who say they cannot be hypnotized are really saying that they will not *allow* themselves to be hypnotized. Thus, if a hypnotist's attempts to hypnotize one of these individuals are unsuccessful and the experience does not produce the hypnosis state, it is not the hypnotist's fault. Allowing oneself to slip into a daydream or to drift off to sleep must occur at a time of one's own choosing, and nobody can be commanded into a relaxed state against his will.

I often tell witnesses with whom I am about to work that they are actually the ones who are going to be doing all the work during a hypnosis session. I compare myself to the role of a coach, and I tell them that if they do not want to do this, then it will not get done.

## *Confidence in the hypnotist*

The last element necessary for someone else to hypnotize a person is that there must be confidence in the hypnotist. If there is no confidence in the hypnotist, the subject might be afraid and will not want to undergo hypnosis. I often use the following analogy during a lecture. Let's say you go to a podiatrist because your foot hurts. After the doctor has examined you, he comes to you with his diagnosis: "There is a definite problem with your foot," he says. "The only solution is to perform brain surgery on you." Of course you would not continue to see a doctor who makes such a diagnosis, and the same holds true for a hypnotist. If you discuss a particular situation with a hypnotist but do not feel at ease with the person, then it is highly unlikely that you will want him to hypnotize you.

It is very important for forensic hypnotists to establish themselves early on as being professional and competent, as a hypnotist may have only one chance to work with a particular witness. During a hypnosis session there must be a rapport between hypnotist and subject. This rapport or bonding must be present in order for the subject to relax enough to go into hypnosis and then undertake the task of attempting to retrieve details pertaining to the crime scene.

These three elements — freedom from fear, willingness, and confidence in the hypnotist — are the crucial elements for a successful hypnosis session. It should be clearer now that hypnosis is not in the hands of the hypnotist, but rather is in those of the subject, and this natural tool is just that — a tool to be used as necessary.

Perhaps another way to understand hypnosis can be found in the formula created by Vince Sheehan, a retired New York police officer and retired instructor of forensic hypnosis at the Ohio Peace Officer's Training Academy in London, Ohio. He explains hypnosis like this:

motivation + expectation + imagination(squared) = hypnosis

This formula summarizes everything we have discussed so far. A person has to *want* to be hypnotized to be hypnotized — that is motivation. We all have certain expectations as to what hypnosis is like, but it is the hypnotist's responsibility to eliminate false expectations of their subjects. By this point, though, it is hoped that any misconceptions that the reader may have had about hypnosis have been dispelled.

In one of several cases using hypnosis that I have had the opportunity to work on, a vehicular homicide incident occurred on a four-lane roadway early in the morning. The person to be hypnotized had been walking next to the victim in the case just before she was struck. After explaining hypnosis and using the induction technique, I asked the witness to go back to the incident and to describe all of the detail she could about what took place. After several moments, the witness opened her eyes and said this was not working. I brought her out of hypnosis and asked her what she had expected. She said she thought she would go to sleep, and when she woke up I would tell her what she had described to me. She expected hypnosis to be like a deep sleep, where she was not aware of anything, even though I had been careful to describe the actual state of hypnosis to her. Because her expectation was not met, though, the session failed.

It is very important to find out what your subject believes hypnosis is like. If they have an image similar to that of the witness in the case described above, then it might be a good idea to use some examples (such as the book and balloon) to explain more fully what hypnosis is actually like.

Then there is perhaps the most important part of the Sheehan formula — imagination (squared). The imagination plays a powerful role in taking mere words from the hypnotist and transforming those into images that the conscious mind can hold for a period of time. In the book-and-balloon exercise, it was the imagination that was able to create the balloon and book and then to allow those images to move an arm up or down. That is imagination (squared).

While the Sheehan formula includes all the ingredients that go into hypnosis, it does not spell out the *secret* of hypnosis, which I have touched on earlier in this chapter — suggestion. While suggestion is a powerful tool to use to achieve a hypnotic state, it is also something the forensic hypnotist needs to be wary of, because the wrong suggestion could lead to the witness' testimony not being admissible in court. This will be discussed later in the forensic hypnosis section.

Returning to discussion at the beginning of this chapter, how would you describe hypnosis to someone? Are you confident in the ability of the examples given here to allay a person's fears of hypnosis? What descriptive words would you use in your explanation?

As we now know, hypnosis is not sleep. It can be described as an altered state of consciousness where concentration, relaxation, and imagination are able to produce a response we call hypnosis. This tool, if used properly, can aid us in many areas of life, not just with the solving of crimes. But to use it to its fullest potential, we must understand more about it.

# chapter two

# History of hypnosis

When was hypnosis discovered and how? In the first chapter, we discussed the fact that we all go through a state of hypnosis at least twice a day — once before waking up and again before drifting off to sleep. This fact alone should tell you about the origin of hypnosis; it has been a part of us since the beginning of time. Like many things about our body, it is just taking us some time to figure out what it is and how we can use it to our benefit.

One of the earliest examples of hypnosis being used can be found in the tribal ceremonies of early humans. Members of a tribe, few in number, were dependent on each other, so when one of them got sick or injured the entire tribe was concerned. The shaman or witch doctor was summoned to cure the disease or heal the injury. While the patient rested in his hut with a small fire or candle to light the room, the village would initiate a healing ceremony. Whether they started with drums or a chant, there was usually some kind of musical prelude. The patient listened to their chants or drum beats and began to be lulled into a relaxed state. Awaiting the arrival of the shaman, the patient's expectations of his healing powers were high; after all, the shaman was one of the most respected members of the tribe and held great power. At the appropriate moment, the shaman would appear in the hut. Dressed from head to foot in his best healing gear, he would perform a ritual to restore the patient's health. When he had exhausted all of his abilities, he would leave.

This is a simple look at a ritual that was very complex and important to these ancient cultures, but it shows that early humans were aware of the power of hypnosis even if they did not know exactly what it was. From what you have read so far in this book, let's analyze this situation to see the role played by hypnosis.

Remember the Sheehan formula? *Motivation* was the first part. In our scenario, not only is the patient motivated to get better, but the entire village or tribe is also behind the patient's efforts. Because the members of the tribe rely on each other so much, everyone is highly motivated to undertake the ceremony. The patient certainly wants to go through with the ceremony, believing that he will get better if he does. This brings us to *expectation* — everyone expects the outcome to be a healed patient. There is no *fear*, because the patient believes in the ability of the shaman to heal. So when the shaman appears in all his splendor, the patient relaxes and allows his imagination to go where directed by the shaman. Because the shaman is so well respected, the patient and the entire tribe have great confidence in his abilities.

Add all this up, and you have the Sheehan formula for hypnosis, as well as the three elements necessary for hypnosis to take place. Early humans knew how to use hypnosis and passed this ability down through the ages. It did not receive a name until much later, however. One of the earliest recorded descriptions of hypnosis was found in an Egyptian tomb written on a piece of papyrus dating back to around 1500 B.C. On this papyrus is explained the method for hypnosis, in much the same manner as that used today. The Egyptians used hypnosis for both religious and medical purposes and passed their knowledge of hypnosis to the Greeks and Romans. Although the early Egyptians did not call it hypnosis, they did associate it with sleep and named it "temple sleep".

Later, a Roman named Esculapius used hypnosis to place his patients into a deep sleep. Once they were in this state, he was able to relieve their pain. Esculapius took the process a step further and began healing his patients by placing his hands on them. Even the Father of Medicine, Hippocrates, acknowledged that hypnosis existed and seemed to work.

In the Far East, recorded uses of hypnosis date back to the formation of many of the Eastern religions. Many of these religions utilize some form of hypnosis in the ceremonies even today. Medicine men in Africa utilized hypnosis for good and evil by using it as a cure (much like our earlier example) or as a curse, as exemplified by the practice of voodoo.

In fact, examples of hypnosis are found in all civilizations in some form or another. The use of suggestion has been a part of many medical and religious practices since early humans — kings and pharaohs have believed they were decedents of the divine because they could heal others with just a touch in ceremonies that resemble hypnosis practices today, with the final step being the placing of hands to heal the person.

As time progressed, the use of hypnosis and its techniques took a backward turn. Physicians turned from the practices of their earlier counterparts, calling them barbaric, and looked elsewhere for solutions. This rejection caused hypnosis to become linked with evil forces during the Dark Ages. Anyone caught practicing hypnosis was branded a witch or warlock. They were hunted down, tried, and convicted of this crime. Hypnosis was driven underground, surfacing later in traveling shows where its techniques were used by stage hypnotists who kept the knowledge alive.

An Austrian physician named Franz Anton Mesmer stumbled onto hypnosis once again in the eighteenth century. He is credited with its "discovery". Mesmer believed that all of us are surrounded by a magnetic field and that for everything in life there is an opposite. He carried this theory with him into his medical practice, speculating that if someone became ill the cure lay not in the science of the day but rather in re-aligning that person's magnetic field. He believed that a person's magnetic field was altered in some way when he became ill.

The conservative Austrian medical community quickly criticized Mesmer for these theories. Mesmer had to flee his homeland to continue to practice his medicine, but he found a receptive audience in France. Mesmer was quite the showman. He would fill a large barrel with water into which he placed magnetic rods. He claimed that this process would magnetize the water. Then he would have a patient step into the barrel. Once the patient was in the barrel, Mesmer called out to him to be healed. The patient would then exit the barrel, feeling fresh and healed.

Once word spread of this new healing technique, Mesmer became very popular. His patients became too numerous to handle on an individual basis. He purchased an estate and began holding healing ceremonies each evening that became the talk of the town. Musicians played soft, soothing music as people gathered in the flickering candlelight. The anticipation of the crowd grew as time passed and the musicians continued to play, while the candles cast a soft light over the tableau, which included a larger version of the original barrel that could hold several people. When all was in place and the moment just right, Mesmer would suddenly appear.

His manner of dress had changed by now. Instead of the clothes of the period, he wore long, flowing gowns adorned with astrological symbols. Around his neck he wore a large magnet bound by a chain. As he strolled through the crowd, shaking hands and waving his magnet over them, he assured his followers that they would find peace and health in his care. In some instances, his patients threw themselves into convulsions after he passed them.

Once he completed his rounds with the crowd, Mesmer would walk to the barrel of magnetic water and begin his procedure. His patients stepped into the water and explained what was bothering them. Mesmer waved his magnet over them to re-magnetize them. For some special cases, Mesmer even had magnets in the shape of the organ or body part that was ailing. He placed these magnets over the affected organs to heal them.

Again, based on what we have discussed so far, you probably see that Mesmer had not really discovered anything new. The soft music, the candles burning, the great expectations — all the same elements were present as for the medicine men's ceremonies of an earlier time and today's hypnotists.

Mesmer did not stop there, though. He soon discovered that he did not need the water and magnetic rods. He found that he could magnetize the water and have the patient drink the water to get better. This evolved into the belief that it was not the magnets or the water at all that were curing the sick. He came to believe that he was gifted with a sort of animal magnetism. He found that all he needed to do was to touch people and they would be healed.

Mesmer eventually found himself in the role of court physician for King Louis XVI. Thanks to this very high-profile position, Mesmer's methods once again were subject to the scrutiny and skepticism of his fellow professionals. An investigation of Mesmer's animal magnetism theory was conducted. Two members of this investigating committee were Benjamin Franklin and Antoine-Laurent Lavoisier, who concluded that there was no basis for Mesmer's belief that there is a magnetic field around the body. They stated further that Mesmer's patients recovered from their illnesses because of their imagination rather than from any type of animal magnetism.

This marked the beginning of the end for Mesmer. Shortly after the investigation, Mesmer found himself again discredited. The French Revolution followed, and Mesmer fled the country. To his last days, though, Mesmer still clung to his belief in animal magnetism. Mesmer is credited with the discovery of hypnosis because of his work. His name also gave us the term "mesmerize", a term used to describe his patients' reactions to his methods. His mode of treatment also came to be known as "mesmerism".

Mesmer was not without his followers. Others learned of his efforts and developed his techniques further. Chastenet de Puysegur, a nobleman of the time, magnetized a tree on his estate and urged peasants to go to the tree when they felt tired and weak so they could gain strength and return to work. By requesting this of his peasants, he hoped to get more work out of them and less illness.

In 1734, a German physician named Maxmillian Hell presented a dissertation on the effects of animal magnetism. He even included the use of organ-shaped magnets as part of the therapy. A Portuguese monk in 1784 was able to utilize Mesmer's theories to treat those who came to him in need, but he finally concluded that there was no such thing as a magnetic fluid or field. In India in 1820, a physician utilized Mesmer's techniques to place his patients into a trance-like state. What he found was that the use of anesthesia declined, as well as the mortality of his patients.

Now that hypnosis was being examined by doctors open to new ideas, progress in understanding this phenomenon slowly moved forward. An English physician, John Elliotson, was able to use Mesmer's principles to place his patients under hypnosis and not administer any anesthesia during operations. He found that during these procedures his patients felt no pain, no matter how extensive the operation. He also discovered that this technique worked very well with patients who had nerve disorders. In another part of the world, another physician was recording similar successes. James Esdaile, a doctor in Calcutta, had the same results as Elliotson. Although the two never compared notes or shared their research, they both found hypnosis to be very effective.

Esdaile, Elliotson, and Mesmer all had something else in common. All of them were criticized by the medical community for their practices. The very thought of something called "animal magnetism" being a part of the scientific community was unthinkable. Their research and successes were quickly dismissed as being nothing more than parlor tricks and frauds.

At this point in history it looked as if hypnosis would be lost, as it was being used for nothing more than side-show attractions and the scientific community had turned its back. Not until 1840 would the development of hypnosis take a new twist. James Braid was doing research into the accomplishments of other physicians. He came upon the animal magnetism theory of Mesmer and those who supported him. Braid agreed with the results of the investigation by Franklin's committee — there was no magnetic field around the human body and thus no animal magnetism. What Braid did find in his own research, though, was a trance-like state that resembled sleep. He found that if someone entered this form of sleep they became very suggestible. Braid knew he was onto something, but he did not want it to be classified with Mesmer. Braid gave this state a new name which remains with us even today. As we have already noted, he drew upon the Greek word for sleep (*hypnos*) to name his discovery "hypnosis".

Although distanced from mesmerism, Braid's hypnosis began a new debate in the medical community. For the first time hypnosis was being seriously considered by legitimate physicians. Braid continued his research and soon learned that what he had theorized about hypnosis was wrong. It was not a sleeping state at all. He found that the person was very much awake and aware of what was taking place around them. Now he decided to change the name of hypnosis to "monoideism" because of the one-on-one association between hypnotist and client. It was too late, though. The name "hypnosis" stuck.

Now that hypnosis was being discussed in a positive light by the medical community, Braid's discovery led others to validate his work. In Strasbourg, a professor named Hippolyte Bernheim described hypnosis as being a psychological process, not physical or physiological. He based his conclusions on his own work and that of Ambroise-Auguste Liebeault. Jean-Martin Charcot of the Sorbonne in Paris developed his own theory of hypnosis. He decided that it was only able to occur in people who suffered from hysteria and parted with Bernheim and Liebeault when he concluded that hypnosis was a pathological state. He went even further and maintained Mesmer's belief that there was reason to believe that magnets and metals play a role in the hypnosis process. His assertions raised the old doubts about hypnotism previously associated with Mesmer.

Then a man named Sigmund Freud appeared on the scene. While on a trip to France, Freud was able to observe hypnosis in use. He was quite impressed with the effects it had in treating individuals who suffered from neurotic disorders. Freud returned to his practice with this new information and immediately put it to use. At the same time he began using hypnosis at his practice in Vienna, he was also developing his psychoanalysis theory. Freud became frustrated with hypnosis when he found that he could not place everyone under hypnosis successfully. As he gained confidence in his new theory of psychoanalysis, Freud discarded the use of hypnosis. By doing so he set the hypnosis research community into a tailspin, as both his popularity and integrity drew a lot of attention toward psychoanalysis at the expense of hypnosis.

Hypnosis was again driven back to the realm of carnivals and entertainment. Its potential was once more forgotten by the medical community in general. All was not lost for hypnosis, though. In 1892, the British Medical Association (BMA) made a bold statement when it formally recognized that hypnosis had applications in modern medicine. In making this claim, the BMA stood apart from the rest of the Western medical communities, who claimed that hypnosis was nothing more than entertainment or had links to mysticism.

When World War I broke out, hypnosis was returned to active duty by the medical community. Doctors found that it could be used very successfully to treat soldiers who suffered from combat neuroses. It was also used to replace anesthetics when those supplies were low. This practice, although not widely discussed, was carried on by the medical community even into World War II. There are many stories from both wars of people who were able to overcome incredible injures with the use of hypnosis. One example is the soldier who lost one of his legs. Knowing that the injury was life threatening, he placed himself under hypnosis and imagined a tourniquet being placed around the leg. He was able to slow the bleeding by telling himself he was stopping the flow of blood to the arteries and veins in his leg. When medical assistance arrived, he was able to receive proper treatment and survived his ordeal.

Another example can be found in a later war. A soldier was captured and placed in a bamboo cage only large enough for him to sit in. To keep his muscles strong and to fight the effects of inactivity, he placed himself into a state of hypnosis. While in hypnosis, he played golf each day, his favorite course from back home, all 18 holes, stroke by stroke. When he was released, many were amazed to find him in good physical shape despite his captivity.

In the U.S., Morton Prince made some discoveries that returned hypnosis to scientific scrutiny. He found that there was a separation of mental systems in people who suffered from the illness termed multiple personality disorder and in people who were in a state of hypnosis. Prince was able to show that when hypnotized a person could actually conduct two or more separate mental processes at the same time. His theories were corroborated by Pierre Janet in France.

The Western world was not alone in its quest for knowledge about hypnosis. Ivan Pavlov, the Russian scientist famous for his bell and dog experiment, also looked into hypnosis. He concluded that hypnosis did resemble sleep, but he also added that there was more to it. He said that during the "sleep" of hypnosis there continued to be neural excitation. Pavlov's theory was widely accepted in Russia and in Eastern Europe, where doctors used hypnosis in their psychiatric therapy with varied success.

In 1933, an American named Clark Hull researched the work of Bernheim. Hull, conducted his own study into hypnosis, and agreed with Bernheim that hypnosis is a state of hyper-suggestibility. Hull's work inspired others to continue to look at this phenomenon scientifically. What was found was there was nothing mystical about hypnosis at all. There was no need for magnets or metal. It was not sleep. It was an altered state of consciousness in which the mind was open to suggestion.

In the 1940s, Milton Erickson took a clinical-experimental approach to hypnosis as he furthered Hull's research. His findings, along with those of Hull's, were able to bring hypnosis out of the entertainment and mystical arena and into a scientific one. Erickson's research led to a complete study of hypnosis now called Ericksonian hypnosis.

Then, in a major breakthrough for hypnosis, the American Medical Association (AMA) declared hypnosis to be a useful medical tool. This was proclaimed in 1958, more than a half century after the BMA had made the same claim. Once it was decided that hypnosis had medical potential, the AMA moved to restrict total use of hypnosis to their members, and they declared it a new discovery.

The AMA was not successful in their attempt to control the study and use of hypnosis. The very people who had been keeping hypnosis alive through the years argued that hypnosis was not a new discovery, but had been with us since the beginning of time. Their arguments won out, and the AMA had to allow others to study and practice hypnosis.

Today hypnosis can be found in many areas and goes by many names. Terms such as *visualization, relaxation therapy,* and *image therapy,* among others, are merely other names for hypnosis. No matter what it is called, hypnosis has been with us always and remains ready to serve our needs.

# chapter three

# Applications of hypnosis

## Types of hypnosis

Even though it goes by only one name, hypnosis actually has three applications, each with a different perspective and different rules for the hypnotist to follow — forensic hypnosis, clinical hypnosis, and stage hypnosis (see Figure 3.1). The forensic hypnotist, more than either of the other kinds of hypnotists, needs to have an understanding of each application and how it is applied. The reason for this is to prepare the forensic hypnotist for the day he finds himself sitting in the witness chair and the defense attorney is preparing to cross-examine. Hypnotists finding themselves in a court situation will also find that hypnosis itself is being placed on trial, as well as the credibility of the hypnotist himself. A complete understanding of how hypnosis works, where it can be applied, and how it can be applied will go a long way toward keeping your integrity intact. The opposition will bring in their own expert (you should expect no less), but if their expert is not a forensic hypnotist then you will want to be able to discuss how the forensic application of hypnosis is different from the forms other experts use.

Because of the very nature of hypnosis, the more the forensic hypnotist understands and can explain, the better off the jury will be to make an educated decision based on truth rather than misconceptions about hypnosis. Let's take a brief look at each form of hypnosis to help understand their differences.

### Stage hypnosis

Hypnosis as seen on the stage has led to many of the myths and misconceptions associated with it. On the stage and in side-shows are where many of the images for the media were forged (see Figure 3.2). Tabloids, novelists, and scriptwriters have often found hypnosis to be a part of the dark side of humanity, often casting the hypnotist in the role of a villain who uses

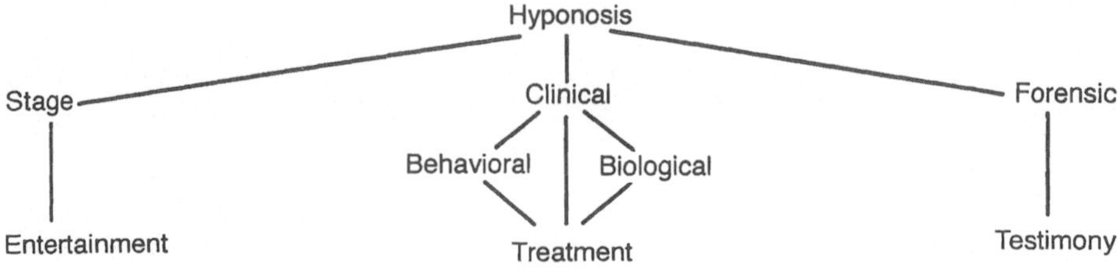


**Figure 3.1** Various types of hypnosis.

hypnosis as a mind-control technique. Such a perception is fine for moving a story line along or creating sensational headlines to sell copies of a newspaper, which is exactly what stage hypnosis gears itself towards: entertainment.

What I am calling stage hypnosis here covers not only what is used in various acts performed live, but also the portrayal of hypnosis in other entertainment media. Is stage hypnosis bad? No, as long as it is understood that what is being shown is for entertainment and is not a representative demonstration of hypnosis. Take the subject of magic, for instance. A magician on the stage is there to mystify you with his abilities and allow you to believe in the illusion of his magic. The magic is not real, but it is good fun and entertaining.

**Figure 3.2** The idea that a hypnotist can place someone under his spell with a swinging pendulum or watch is based more on myth than fact.

The stage hypnotist does nothing less than the magician. Up on the stage, the hypnotist wants you to believe all the old stories associated with hypnosis. Why? Because you will enjoy the show more that way. You are entertained, which leads you to tell your friends about the show, and then they will come, and so on. In this manner, the stage hypnotist, like the magician, always has an audience and so they will continue to work.

As long as everyone in the audience understands that the hypnosis displayed up on the stage is just for fun no harm is done. Just as people leaving a show by a famous magician know that he has no real magical abilities, so too should those leaving a stage hypnosis show understand that the hypnosis used is not a true picture of this phenomenon.

It was actually the stage hypnotist that preserved the knowledge and understanding of hypnosis. During the Dark Ages, people who used hypnosis were often mistaken as witches and were subsequently executed. Hypnosis used as a traveling side show for entertainment, though, was not looked upon quite so strictly, which allowed the secrets of hypnosis to survive. In order to entertain someone with hypnosis, the stage hypnotist must understand hypnosis just as much as the other two kinds of hypnotists do; the difference comes in the application of it. Whereas practitioners of the other two applications of hypnosis want to explain away the myths and help clients to understand fully what they are about to do, the stage hypnotist wants to understand hypnosis as much as possible so he can use that knowledge to enhance the entertainment value of his performance.

During a stage hypnosis show, have you ever noticed how the hypnotist does not just come out into the audience and pick two or three people at random to help him do the show? Unless they have assistants planted in the audience, they cannot count on the three people they have picked to be responsive to their suggestions. Remember back to the first chapter and the three elements needed for hypnosis, one of which was freedom from fear. What if one of the three people the hypnotist chose at random is afraid of public speaking or being in front of a live audience? Fear would prevent this person from relaxing to the point of being able to accept suggestions, which would not be good for the show.

What a stage hypnotist will do instead is to ask a group of individuals to come up on the stage. Usually they will want as large a group as the stage will comfortably hold, because the more people they have to choose from the better their chances of getting the right candidate for the show.

Once the volunteers are on the stage, the hypnotist will now begin to offer a group of suggestibility tests, similar to the book-and-balloon example used in Chapter 1. As the hypnotist offers these suggestions, he watches their reactions very carefully. The people who do not respond immediately to his requests are politely tapped on the shoulder and asked to take their seats. Then the hypnotist uses another test and another, until he ends up with two or three people on the stage. This method of picking out audience members has a much greater chance for success than picking people out randomly and helps ensure that the hypnotist will be able to put on a good show.

What makes these few people so different from the others? They all have the three elements necessary to go into a state of hypnosis. They are free from fear and are willing to participate; otherwise, they would not have gone up on the stage in the first place. They also have shown confidence in the hypnotist, because they have accepted the suggestions already offered to them by the hypnotist and have allowed those suggestions to have an effect on them and their bodies.

In essence, what you find up on the stage with the hypnotist are people who deep in their hearts have always wanted to perform in front of a live audience and are there because they want to have a good time. They have no inhibitions about what will be expected of them from the hypnotist; if they did, they would not have reacted as they did to his earlier suggestions. They also know they can act as carefree as they want to on the stage because they have the perfect alibi — they were hypnotized and had no control over their actions. The hypnotist will not dispel this myth, because it is what keeps people coming back. The subject will not dispel it and the audience wants to believe it, because it is this myth that excuses the participants for their actions and provides the entertainment.

This form of hypnosis is great entertainment, but there are problems associated with it as well, because this is the version on which many individuals base their opinions, which is part of what has kept hypnosis in the Dark Ages instead of being used as the modern tool that it is. The stage hypnotist preserving the mysteries surrounding hypnosis and keeping it in the shadows has done as much harm as good to its image and potential.

### *Clinical hypnosis*

Called by many different names, the clinical application of hypnosis is the most heavily practiced form of hypnosis in our society today. Visualization, stress management, image therapy, and other terms all describe treatments that are applications of hypnosis. The technique is not necessarily called hypnosis because of all the questions that would immediately be raised. On the other hand, if a doctor suggested that a patient undergo some "image therapy", the questions are much fewer and the patient is less apprehensive about it.

As the title suggests, clinical hypnosis is the application of hypnosis as a treatment. This is actually the oldest form of hypnosis and the most beneficial to mankind. This use of hypnosis can assist in areas ranging from study habits, quitting smoking, dental work, pain control, and controlling blood pressure to its use in cancer treatments. This simple, natural tool has much potential if the interest to use it is there.

Within the area of clinical hypnosis are two subcategories that describe the use of hypnosis in more detail — behavioral and biological. Each of these categories has different requirements of the hypnotist. Even though the qualities of hypnosis remain constant, the abilities of the hypnotist do not, and the successful practitioner of clinical hypnosis must know the proper application of it.

### *Behavioral hypnosis*

Behavioral hypnosis involves those areas relating to how we act or react to things and events in our life — issues such as test anxiety, smoking, grinding teeth at night, stress management, sports performance, aggressiveness, likability, shyness, self-esteem, and others. The distinction between behavioral and biological hypnosis must be made, as anyone trained in hypnosis can assist someone with a behavioral problem, but the use of hypnosis for biological problems requires a specialist, at least for the initial examination.

One way to distinguish the two aspects of clinical hypnosis is to remember that if we have control over a condition, in any way, then it will fall into the behavioral classification; otherwise, it will be biological in nature. Many people each year seek out a hypnotist to aid them with some aspect of their life. Audio tapes for stress reduction, smoking cessation, and other types of self-help have flooded the market, and, while they usually are not called hypnosis tapes, the techniques used in the tapes to reach the desired goal are in reality forms of hypnosis. College students who find themselves swamped with overwhelming amounts of work and material to be covered have found a hypnotist to be just the teaching aid necessary to help them recall important information on the day of the final examination. Individuals who enroll in a sports clinic, such as tennis, might expect at the end of a session to go through some mental imagery drills in which they see themselves hitting the perfect backhand or crushing a blistering serve. Hypnosis has been of benefit in such situations and many more relating to our behavior.

The success rate for individuals in this area is in direct proportion to how much desire there is on the part of the person being hypnotized. When someone seeks out a hypnotist for one of these areas, they sometimes arrive with the expectation that the hypnotist will make them stop whatever habit they are trying to break. The problem is, a hypnotist cannot force someone to do something against his will. They can make suggestions for the individual to change his ways and help those suggestions slip into the subconscious mind, but the hypnotist cannot *make* anyone do anything.

An illustration of this point can be found in the example of a person who wants to stop smoking. This is a common reason for people to seek out a hypnotist. For some it only takes a few sessions, and they find themselves smoke free. There are even those who need only one session. Others, however, find that they can resist smoking for only a short time before they go back to their old habits. Why does hypnosis have such a varied success rate? The answer lies more with the person undergoing hypnosis than with the hypnosis itself. Remember that the only thing a hypnotist can do is offer suggestions, words, and phrases that each individual must accept and decide what to do with. It is like having a coach standing beside you telling you that you can perform to your best ability, that you can overcome the opposition. That voice (the suggestions) will only have an effect on you if you allow it to.

Let's look at this a little more in depth. If you want to quit a habit such as smoking, you have to really want to do it in order to overcome not only the addiction to nicotine but also the habit of smoking at certain times of the day, such as with your morning coffee, after a meal, on a break at work, while socializing, and so forth. If you are trying to quit smoking because your significant other wants you to and you do not really want to, then even with hypnosis you are doomed to failure. The reason is sooner or later you will find an excuse to have another one. It could be something as simple as a stressful day that drives you to have one, just one, to ease your stress. That one will lead to another and another, even if you have managed to quit for several days, weeks, or even months. A friend of mine who was able to quit smoking said he used the following thought to keep himself focused on breaking his habit: "I'm only a puff away from a pack a day." He was able to quit because he set his mind to it, but, just like hypnosis, no one can make you do something if you do not really want to.

So, when smokers seek out the help of a hypnotist, the ones who succeed are usually the ones who truly want to quit, because they have made up their minds that they are going to do it and have put forth the effort. A posthypnotic suggestion only lasts a few days anyway, so the suggestions a hypnotist offers will not be with you the next week unless you reinforce those suggestions. Really, after the first session, you are on your own as far as breaking a habit. A person who does not really want to quit but goes to a hypnotist often wants the hypnotist to command them to quit. When they discover that they still want to smoke, the usual response is that hypnosis did not work and they continue their habit.

The will of the human spirit is very strong, and there is no person who can force someone to break a habit without the cooperation of that person. The use of hypnosis can only aid the will in the breaking of a habit; it cannot replace the will.

Hypnosis has had excellent results with individuals in many areas of behavior and can become an excellent resource to help during difficult times. I have had the opportunity to work with several individuals in relation to test anxiety and have found that with a short session many of these anxieties can be put aside. An example is an officer who was preparing for the sergeants' examination. The examination was a two-part test comprised of a written exam followed by an assessment center. This particular officer came to me for help with the assessment center part. The suggestions given to him were basically ego strengthening to help bolster his confidence because the assessment center throws the officer into the arena against fellow co-workers, which is quite stressful. I made him an audio tape and he listened to it just prior to the testing process. When the results of the assessment center were released, this particular officer found himself in first place. Did the hypnosis do that? No, *he* did it; the hypnosis only helped him to be as good as he could be, which is what hypnosis is used for in behavioral situations. It will not make you something you are not; it will only help you be the best you.

### *Biological hypnosis*

As the name implies, biological hypnosis is hypnosis applied to matters concerning our bodies. Areas such as pain control, weight loss, sexual dysfunction, psychosis, neurosis, bed wetting, and others are all included in this classification of hypnosis. There is a stipulation for this area that hypnotists must follow: Because the very nature of this type of treatment involves the medical profession, before a hypnotist can perform hypnosis for a biological ailment, he must first have approval from a physician in the field relating to that particular problem. Unless the hypnotist is trained as a doctor as well, they cannot treat a patient, because that would be practicing medicine without a license.

Let's look at a couple of examples to help illustrate the reasoning behind this restriction. Pain management is an area in which hypnosis has had some remarkable achievements. Throughout its history there have been reported cases, usually from war-time settings, where hypnosis was used when no anesthesia was available, and the results were successful. There was even a story told to me while I was attending an advanced class on forensic hypnosis. A solider during World War II was hit by mortar fire, and his arm was severed. Fearing he would bleed to death before help could arrive, he mentally placed a valve on his severed arm and began to turn it so that the valve was shut. When the medics were able to reach him, his bleeding was slowed enough that they were able to save his life. Whether this story is true or not I cannot say, but it is similar to many stories I have heard regarding the success of hypnosis during drastic times. I personally had the opportunity to see some relief offered by hypnosis to someone who was suffering from cancer. An officer's wife was fighting a cancer that was very resistant to any type of treatment, and her husband agreed to let me try hypnosis to give her some relief. During my initial interview with her, a chronic cough constantly interrupted her when she tried to speak. I then proceeded with the session and kept her in hypnosis for about 30 minutes. When the session ended, the officer commented that during those 30 minutes he noticed that his wife did not cough once. This was the first time in a long time that she had been able to do that. Her mind was able to overcome her affliction during that short period of time because she allowed herself to slip into a relaxed state and concentrate on the suggestions offered.

Pain was given to us for a reason, however, and because of this the hypnotist must be careful when working with someone who wants it removed. An example is a person who might come to a hypnotist because they are suffering from headaches. With the aid of suggestions, headaches can be relieved (even migraines), but the risk comes when there is a biological reason for those headaches, such as a tumor. Until a medical doctor is able to verify that there is not a medical condition causing the pain, the hypnotist and the subject are playing a deadly game with pain removal. The patient's pain could be relieved for awhile, but in time an unchecked tumor could grow too large for the patient to be saved by his doctors. This is why the hypnotist needs to have a doctor examine the patient first before any type of pain removal is performed. Hypnosis is not a medical cure but an aid.

Another common use for hypnosis is to aid with weight loss. Many people each year seek out various methods to help them lose unwanted pounds; in fact, the health and weight-loss industries are the largest in our society today. Most weight problems are the direct result of our own habits. We eat too much and exercise too little. As age creeps up on us, we find that our tummies, legs, and rear ends are not what they once were. This may be the case for the majority of individuals who find themselves overweight, but there are still people who unfortunately can do all the right things and still have a weight problem. These people suffer from such medical conditions as an overactive thyroid. Because of this possibility, a hypnotist must have his client seek out a medical doctor before using hypnosis for weight loss. Unless a hypnotist is qualified to make the determination that there is no biological reason for the excess weight, he must send his client to someone who can. This will ensure the safety of the client and the hypnotist's practice.

A simple rule to follow is if the problem can be related to our bodies in any way, physically or mentally, and is not merely a habit, then a person needs to seek out a qualified medical professional before seeking the assistance of a hypnotist. A hypnotist who is ethical will not overstep his limits and will refer someone to a health professional if the problem is biological. Among the many possibilities for hypnosis in the future, this particular area shows great promise. As was mentioned earlier in this book, such hypnosis is being called many names, such as image therapy and visualization exercises, but the technique is hypnosis nonetheless.

## *Forensic hypnosis*

Forensic hypnosis is the use of hypnosis for investigative purposes in both civil and criminal cases and for both the prosecutor and the defense. It is primarily utilized to enhance a witness' memory. Because the second part of this book will cover hypnosis used for criminal cases on behalf of law enforcement, that discussion will not be held at any length here. There are many guidelines and procedures to be followed for the use of hypnosis by law enforcement, which will be explained in more detail.

The difference between forensic hypnosis and the other categories of hypnosis is that there is a specific goal — the gathering of information regarding a specific incident. When the forensic hypnotist goes to work, whether on a civil or criminal case, he is charged with the task of helping the client refresh his memory and come up with details that will aid in the case.

The admissibility of the testimony from these hypnosis sessions depends on each court. (The admissibility of hypnosis testimony in criminal court proceedings will be discussed in a later chapter.)

For example, an attorney in a civil case may request that his client undergo a hypnosis session to retrieve vital details that could lead to a possible edge in their case. It could be as simple as remembering who all was in the room when a verbal agreement was reached or who witnessed the signing of a contract or who was standing around an accident scene and saw what color the light was before the accident. All these and many more possibilities could be sought during a session. The weight of testimony gained in this manner is determined by each court, but it strengthens a case to have evidence backed by confirming testimony.

Defense attorneys in criminal cases can also ask that their clients undergo hypnosis to try to remember more details about an incident. In the introduction to this book was discussed the case of Cornell v. Superior Court of San Diego. This was a case where the defense used hypnosis to aid them in preparing their defense. The same rules apply to the defense as to the police, except for the one key point — law enforcement does not ask suspects to undergo hypnosis. The reason for this will be discussed in greater detail later, but for now it is enough to understand that a person can lie under hypnosis just as well as they can out of hypnosis. Because of this, only the defense will ask their client undergo hypnosis.

Forensic hypnosis can also be distinguished from the other forms as being more narrow in focus and directed to the specific goal of obtaining details about a specific incident.

## *Of titles and things*

Titles are terms that imply importance. We use titles such as doctor, attorney, C.E.O., president, senator, all these and many more every day, but one of the most overused and abused words used to classify a particular practitioner of hypnosis is hypnotherapist. You might not think that this term means very much, but it carries just as much meaning as the titles of psychiatrist vs. psychologist. One of these people is an actual doctor, while the other is highly trained and skilled in psychology. The one you go to depends on your condition. The same thing applies to titles for hypnotists.

As the term implies, a hypnotherapist is a person trained in hypnosis who is also qualified to offer therapy. In order to offer therapy, a person must be skilled in areas other than hypnosis, and to do that they must earn a college degree in a field of study such as counseling, with the minimum degree obtained being a Masters. Or, the hypnotherapist may be a fully trained psychologist or psychiatrist.

Now, go to the telephone book and open up the Yellow Pages. Look under the hypnosis heading. You are going to find plenty of listings for individuals calling themselves hypnotherapists. The problem is that the majority of these individuals are merely people who have been trained in hypnosis and are able to obtain more business by calling themselves hypnotherapists. This is a disservice to the client, because such hypnotists are not really able to offer the kind of assistance this person is seeking. Again, it is like seeing the wrong kind of specialist.

Hypnosis training is the same for everyone. There are no accredited universities that offer degrees in hypnosis. Those who want to learn hypnosis must seek out private schools to acquire this training. This is important to note because it also means that the doctors and therapists who use hypnosis in their work are trained exactly the same way as the other people who use hypnosis, including the stage hypnotist. We often give extra importance to someone who holds a degree, and in regard to the subject of their degree they have put forth effort and should be given some credibility for doing so. But, a police officer trained in hypnosis is just as knowledgeable on the subject of hypnosis as a psychiatrist and psychologist. In fact, the Ohio Supreme Court recognized this point and even went on to say in State v. Weston that if an officer is qualified and competent in matters of hypnosis it does not matter if they are not a psychologist or psychiatrist. The reason for this is they underwent the very same training in hypnosis. Hypnosis courses cover only the subject of hypnosis and not therapy; the reverse is true of therapy courses in that they do not cover the application and instruction of hypnosis.

So what term is applied to someone who is merely trained in hypnosis but does not hold a qualifying degree so they can call themselves hypnotherapist? There are several, but they all mean the same — hypnosis consultant, hypnotechnician, and hypnotist. These terms all refer to the lay hypnotist, so if you look in the telephone book and find listings under one of these titles you will know that they can aid you with hypnosis the same as a "hypnotherapist" except in the areas where you need to consult a physician first. The question may then come up as to how one knows if the person using hypnosis is qualified and competent. The answer could be in the area of certification.

## Certification

At the present time there are no governing or licensing agencies for hypnosis, which creates a "buyer beware" sort of situation for the public. Anyone can take a course in hypnosis and place their name and number in the yellow pages and begin to receive clients, even though they may not be competent. The only badge of competence offered at the present time is hypnosis associations that offer certification.

There are usually several tests the applicant must undergo before certification is granted. The first is usually a written examination containing questions about hypnosis theories, history, applications, and ethics. Once passing the written examination, the applicant will then usually face a board of certified hypnotists who will ask them questions, face to face. These questions may be similar to the written exam and will often cover other topics or situations more in-depth. With these two tests, an association can be fairly sure of the qualifications the applicants have and their grasp of the material which will enable them to move onto the third test, where a case study is usually presented to the applicants and the applicants will have to demonstrate how they would handle this particular client under the watchful eye of the certified hypnotists.

Before the applicants are able to undergo these tests, there is usually a requirement that they have a minimum number of college credit hours in the field of psychology or be able to pass a test on the subject of psychology. They must also have taken hypnosis from an acceptable school and have practiced hypnosis for a set amount of time (usually the minimum is a year) before they can apply for certification.

At the present time, the certification is the highest recognition a hypnotist can achieve. Of course, the certification awarded is only as good as the organization offering the certification, and unfortunately there is no way for the public to really know a good organization from one that merely wants the applicants to pay for their certificates. This may change in the future, but right now certification remains the only badge of competence.

There are some organizations who are offering degrees in hypnosis in an effort to gain their students more respectability, but it should be noted that no accredited university offers such a degree, and the amount of emphasis placed on these papermill diplomas should be minimal. A simple thought offered by the Association to Advance Ethical Hypnosis may sum up this section on certification: You do not have to be certified to be competent, but you do have to be competent to be certified.

# *chapter four*

# *The three laws of suggestibility*

Three basic laws or principles of suggestion to be followed when using hypnosis allow the hypnotist to understand how the human mind works so that the hypnotic session will be more productive. These three laws are the Law of Concentrated Attention, the Law of Reversed Effect, and the Law of Dominant Effect. Each will be discussed here briefly.

## *The Law of Concentrated Attention*

This law of suggestion says simply that the more we concentrate on something, the more likely it is that something will happen. This may best be explained by way of examples. Imagine that you are driving your car down a road and you see a pothole on one side of the road. You know that it is a pothole, you do not want to hit the pothole, and you concentrate on the pothole knowing that you want to avoid it. As you approach it, you find to your disgust that you still hit the pothole despite not wanting to. Has this ever happened to you or someone you know? The reason for hitting the pothole is that you have focused your attention on the pothole. True, you want to avoid that pothole, but you are concentrating on it. Because of this concentration, you move toward the object almost subconsciously and your concern about hitting the pothole becomes reality.

Another example can be found in radio and television commercials. These commercials are played over and over so that you, the consumer, will have that particular name brand or service fixed firmly inside your head when you go to the store. When you shop, the commercial tends to influence the type of product you purchase. For example, you are likely to purchase a name-brand cereal because it is supposed to taste better, even though you have compared the ingredients of both the name brand cereal and a generic brand and found that they contain the same things. By hearing the same commercial over and over again we are influenced to concentrate on that product when we do our shopping.

Have you ever worried about something so much that it came true? Take, for instance, the first time you had to give a speech. You might have been worried that you would say a wrong word or forget part of the speech, and when it came time to actually do the speech, you did exactly what you were worried about. Remember the first time you stood at home plate and faced a pitched ball in baseball? You might have imagined that you were going to strike out, only to discover that is exactly what you did. These examples all illustrate some unfortunate results of the law of concentrated attention, but think of the possibilities if you could focus your attention on only good things happening.

Let's look at a particular real-life example of this law in practice. A daredevil named Karl Wallenda used to do all sorts of fantastic feats while walking wires at great heights. All his life he concentrated on getting across the wire safely. His total mindset was making it across the wire, except for one time. On his last walk, he expressed to some that he had a fear of falling. When he made that walk, he did slip and fall to his death. The mind is a very powerful tool, and a hypnotist must know how it works to be effective.

## *The Law of Reversed Effect*

The second law of suggestion, the Law of Reversed Effect, has probably been experienced by all of us at one time or another. This law says that the harder you try to do something the more likely you will not be able to do it. An example of this could be when you encounter someone you know, perhaps a person you knew a long time ago or simply someone you have met before. You try to recall their name but find that you cannot. You know that you know the name, but you cannot bring it to your conscious mind. Then, when the person has left and you relax, perhaps even hours later, the name suddenly comes to mind. This is an example of the Law of Reversed Effect. In this example, you tried to recall the name right away but could not. Your will tried to force your mind to remember, but now the mind is thinking about how it cannot remember the name. A conflict ensues, but the imagination is even stronger than our will. The name eludes you because you are *imagining* that you cannot remember the name, no matter how much you are *willing* the name to be forced out. Only later when the imagination has settled down does the name come to mind.

Another example of this law can be found in sports. A baseball is hit to a fielder, but the ball hits the heel of his glove and bounces onto the ground. The fielder bends over to try to pick up the ball, only to find that he can't seem to lift it off the ground. The more he tries, the more the ball slips out of his reach, until at last he is able to grasp it in his hand. Has this ever happened to you or someone you know? This is an example of a reversed effect.

This law plays a major role in habit breaking. People who smoke, eat too much, or are hooked on any type of behavior say that they want to quit. Their wills tell them that they want to quit and they *can* quit. But, back deep in their minds, the imagination can only see them continuing on with the habit. The end result is that the person continues their habits. The imagination will always be stronger than the will.

This law works with the Law of Concentrated Attention when a person imagines himself either failing or succeeding at something. Take the example of the person giving the speech. If, in his mind, he can see himself getting up there and forgetting part of the speech, then most likely he will do just that. The reverse is also true — when the person can see himself standing up at the podium delivering a flawless performance he is likely to do just that. The imagination will win out.

A famous and very successful ice hockey player is Wayne Gretzky. Many ice hockey players going after a goal say they are trying to shoot the puck *past* the goal-tender, only to have the goal-tender block the shot most of the time. Wayne Gretzky's philosophy, on the other hand, has never been to shoot the puck past the goal-tender, but rather to look for the open parts of the net and shoot the puck toward those spots. His philosophy has gained him the status of being one of the all-time great hockey players.

If you see a particular outcome in your mind, this will most likely be the result when you really do perform the task. Clinical hypnotists learn to use this law to their advantage to help clients. Examples of hypnosis being used in sports can be found in increasing numbers. Tennis clinics are employing the use of "visual imagery" after a tennis session, when the students are asked to picture in their minds performing a particular technique perfectly.

Thinking negative or positive thoughts on a consistent basis is how we program ourselves, but keep in mind that the imagination will always have more influence over our lives than do our wills.

## *The Law of Dominant Effect*

According to this law, a strong emotion will take the place of a weaker one. Say you are having a nice time visiting with some friends. You are talking and enjoying their company. Then you suddenly smell smoke and realize that a fire has broken out and is blocking your escape from the building. Danger is a strong emotion. The stronger emotion will replace the weaker emotion of pleasure because your conscious mind will try to survive what it is up against. It must make danger a priority, so all of your attention becomes focused on the problem before you.

Fear, pain, and danger are not always the stronger emotions, though. Remember back to when you were a child and you fell down and scraped your knee, or perhaps you slipped and skinned your hands trying to break your fall. You ran to the one person who you knew could take care of you — your mother. Your mother would look at the injury, wipe your tears away, probably clean the wound, and say something like, "Would you like mommy to kiss it and make it better?" Then she would kiss you near the injury, and almost immediately the pain of the incident was pushed aside. In this example, whether your mother knew it or not, she was giving you a suggestion for your brain to say the pain is now going away. The suggestion was strengthened by the touch of her lips. This dual approach allows the mind to accept the suggestion and to let this new comforting emotion replace the pain emotion.

Hypnotists often utilize this approach when working with clients. To assist clients to believe they are walking on a beach, the hypnotist will describe the beach and have the sound of the surf playing on a tape player. The client then not only hears the words describing the beach but also hears the sounds of the ocean. This combination will overcome other thoughts and allow the mind to relax and visualize the setting.

This law is just as important for a hypnotist to understand as the other two because hypnosis is suggestion. An understanding of how different influences affect suggestion is required to gain optimal results from any hypnosis session.

## *The three laws combined*

The man who popularized auto-suggestion, Emile Coué, made full use of these three laws yet never utilized hypnosis as we know it. Coué believed that if we gave ourselves a single suggestion several times a day that suggestion would tend to realize itself. He did not believe the suggestion should be specific, but that it should be a general positive suggestion that could be said with minimal effort but yield optimum results.

He had his patients say this single, positive phrase several times a day and monitored their success. He did not care about the steps in between but was concerned only with the outcome. Word of his successes with auto-suggestion spread throughout the globe. Even today auto-suggestion is being utilized. You may have even used it and not known it.

Coué's most famous line for auto-suggestion is, "Every day in every way I am getting better and better." This simple line repeated over and over again achieved the results that Coué wanted for his clients. Looking at that phrase and considering the three laws of suggestion, do you see any that apply? You should have noticed right away the presence of the Law of Concentrated Attention. The simple phrase is repeated several times a day, just as commercials are played on radio and television. The Law of Reversed Effect is present, as well. Because the phrase is being repeated over and over again, the person will begin to carry out that thought even if he believes otherwise, as the imagination will begin to "see" it. What the mind can see, it will try to carry out. The result is the person begins to feel better and better in all ways. Finally, the Law of Dominant Effect also finds its way into this simple phrase. We hear the suggestion that every day in every way we are getting better and better. It is like a mother telling a child that her kissing his injury will make it feel better. We tell ourselves every day we are going to be better than we were the day before and accept the suggestion. It is another day, so we are going to be better than we were before.

Hypnosis and the power of suggestion have touched our lives in many ways. A hypnotist, especially one who will be testifying in court, has to understand the laws of suggestion to be able to explain them in court, should the occasion arise. As many popular cases have shown, when it comes to forensic science in a court situation the knowledge of the person claiming to be an expert will come under scrutiny. A thorough knowledge of suggestion, which is the key to hypnosis, is a must.

# *chapter five*

# *The feeling of hypnosis*

What does it feel like to be in hypnosis? This is a common question asked of the hypnotist and someone who has been hypnotized. It is our natural curiosity to want to know about something in so much detail before we jump in ourselves. The difficulty in answering such a question is that each of us reacts to things differently; what one person may experience during a session another may not. There are some commonly reported experiences that seem to surface more than others, and those will be discussed here. Keep in mind that if you or someone with whom you discuss hypnosis do not experience the symptoms here, it does not mean that you were not hypnotized or that your reactions were abnormal. The experience of hypnosis is unique for each of us.

For the practicing hypnotist, describing what the client may expect during a hypnosis session will become a routine part of the interview portion of their work. During the interview, one of the things a client is going to want to know is what they can expect out of the session and how it will feel to them. This is when the hypnotist will be able to begin to establish his credibility and to alleviate any fears or misconceptions the client may hold. In Chapter 1, I explained that the subject to be hypnotized must be free of fear and have confidence in the hypnotist, and it is here that the hypnotist will be able to lay the groundwork for a successful session.

One of the things I explain first is that the person will not feel like they are in a trance. You can use the examples found in Chapter 1 to help illustrate this point by showing the person Figures 1.2 and 1.3 so he can visualize how hypnosis will feel. As many times as I have been in hypnosis, I still hear that voice at the back of my head saying that I am not really hypnotized, even though I fully understand that I am. This will probably be true for you and others with whom you work. It is nothing to worry about, because this is a trait of hypnosis common to most people.

When I am in hypnosis an inner voice will talk to me, but I also hear the voice of the hypnotist telling me some suggestions, and I find myself responding to those suggestions. For example, Fran Renner, one of my instructors and a founding member of the Association to Advance Ethical Hypnosis (AAEH), was going through the steps to hypnotize a person and decided to try the entire class. I remember myself sitting in the chair hearing her words and saying to myself that I was not under hypnosis. Then she suggested that my right arm would begin to get lighter and lighter and to rise up to my shoulder. I knew what was asked of me, but at the same time I remember saying to myself that I am only going to do this because I do not want to embarrass Fran. I thought that she might have a tough time with the rest of the class and that if I opened my eyes I would see that everyone else was sitting there with their hands down at their sides. As I was thinking this, my arm began to drift upwards. I knew I was doing this, and I allowed it to happen.

It is difficult sometimes to explain hypnosis, because during hypnosis your conscious mind remains so active. When I discussed this with Fran, she nodded her head while I was offering my experiences. She explained that this was the conscious mind accepting the suggestions. The fact that I justified it to myself was just the conscious mind explaining why the arm was rising. I was in hypnosis and accepted the suggestions, but I was not in a trance. It was her opinion that I was still looking for a trance-like feeling or to feel something different, but with hypnosis all you feel is relaxed.

When explaining this aspect of hypnosis to clients, I ask that even if they do not think they are in hypnosis to just bear with me and go along with the suggestions. This usually works, because when they do not achieve that trance-like feeling they are expecting, they think to themselves that they are not in hypnosis but are playing along with me, as I asked and just as I did with Fran Renner.

One of the most frequently reported experiences from a hypnosis session is the loss of time. When asked how long they were in hypnosis, many report a much shorter time frame than the actual time that passed. What may seem like only 15 minutes to them in actual time was closer to 40 minutes, perhaps even an hour. The concept of time passing quickly is not as difficult to explain as the non-sleep state of hypnosis. Whenever we are totally involved with something, time seems to stand still. Think back to a time when you were working on a project, were watching a sporting event, or were so immersed in some other activity that you were not checking the time. When your involvement was over, was there ever a time that you were surprised by so much time passing? This is where the cliché "time flies when you're having fun" comes from. We are so focused on the activity in front of us that we lose all concept of time. The same thing happens during hypnosis.

During a hypnosis session you become so focused on what the hypnotist is saying that time is not important for you. In effect you stop marking minutes and draw yourself completely into the creative process of the hypnosis imagery. When you emerge from this focused attention, more time is likely to have passed than you were aware of. Test this for yourself. In the next chapter, there is a sample hypnosis session. Before you undertake this exercise, jot down the time on a piece of paper and then forget about the time issue. Follow the instructions for the hypnosis session, and when you have completed it check the time again. You may find that you are in for a surprise!

People often report some slight tingling or numbness, which shows up primarily in the legs, feet, toes, hands, fingers, and scalp. Only one area of tingling is felt at a time, so there is no overall numbness or tingling. There is no discomfort associated with this sensation, as the effect is very slight. If the tingling were to become a distraction, the result would be that the subject loses his focus on the hypnosis suggestions and begins instead to concentrate on the annoying tingling, which would cause him to come out of hypnosis. This could occur if a person sat with his legs or arms crossed, restricting the blood flow when a hypnosis session lasts for a long period of time. The effect I am referring to here, though, is only very slight and would not draw a person out of hypnosis.

Others have described a feeling of lightness or heaviness in various parts of their bodies during hypnosis. This sensation can be a general overall feeling or can be limited to a specific part of the body, such as one of the extremities. This feeling usually is a result of the suggestions offered to the subject by the hypnotist — for example, the book-and-balloon demonstration in Chapter 1, in which the suggestion was offered that the left arm with the balloon tied around it was floating upwards, while the right hand holding a heavy book was sinking. These sensations were most definitely felt by those who allowed it, but there was no discomfort associated with it.

Sometimes with the lightness feeling there is a sensation of floating. You may begin to feel yourself becoming buoyant and think you are going to rise right up out of your seat. That will not physically happen, of course, but the feeling will be there all the same. When I have felt this sensation, it reminds me of being in a pool, holding my breath, sinking under the water, and then ceasing all movement. My body begins to rise up in the water until my back breaks the surface of the water. The feeling is not unpleasant, and I have found that it lasts only a short moment. One way of thinking about this floating sensation is that that during hypnosis a person becomes so relaxed that the pressures of everyday life have been lifted and he begins to feel light and free.

In regard to the sensation of heaviness, I have found from my own experiences and from those who I have hypnotized that the feeling is more like a sinking back into a chair. It is almost as if you sink lower in the chair and can feel it cushion your body. Like the floating sensation, this is not an unpleasant experience and also lasts for a brief period of time during the hypnosis session.

The eyelids may flutter, which is one sensation that the hypnotist will be able to observe during the session. There also can be some tearing or a slight burning feeling in the eyes. Others have described a sensation similar to getting some sand in their eyes, which feels scratchy. I have witnessed a person in hypnosis begin to rub his eyes because of the sensation that something was in his eye. However irritating that might have been, he remained in hypnosis throughout the session. Afterwards, I asked him about the experience and he said that his eyes were irritated but not enough to make him want to leave the feeling of hypnosis.

The mouth can experience a wide range of sensations varying from very dry to very moist. Both types of sensations have been reported, but there have been no studies performed to find out if this is a result of the suggestions being offered by the hypnotist, the topic being discussed, or a biological reaction to the hypnosis.

One of the most obvious sensations is the change in breathing during hypnosis. As the hypnotist begins the induction part of a hypnosis session, he usually tells the subject to take a deep breath and let it out slowly. I have found (especially with people being hypnotized for the first time) that those first breaths are rapid because the subjects are nervous, but as the sessions progress the breathing becomes slower and calmer. This is logical, of course, because when you have drifted off to a daydream your body relaxes and along with that relaxation your breathing has slowed. The breathing also tends to become abdominal-type breathing, which is much deeper and slower than when a person breathes with the upper body only. A person involved in a workout or sports activity tends to take more rapid, shallower breaths than does a completely relaxed person.

Because hypnosis is related so closely to relaxation, the heart rate slows. Today one method to help heart patients is to relieve their stress, and one way of doing this is with relaxation tapes, which may not seem like hypnosis but still have all the attributes of hypnosis. When a person is relaxed, there is less strain on the heart, thus when hypnosis removes the stresses of the day a healthier heart is a result. The relaxation techniques learned through hypnosis can often help patients stay calm and lower their blood pressure when they find themselves under stress.

Another common sensation is to feel perspiration on the palms of your hands and the balls of your feet. This can be influenced by the suggestions given as well. A young lady with whom I had the opportunity to work agreed to go under hypnosis, but she specified that she wanted to "go" to a beach. While I was describing the beach to her and had her walking along the white sand with the sun directly overhead beaming down on her, I noticed perspiration beginning to develop on her upper lip. When she was brought out of hypnosis, she commented that her hands were wet and she felt very warm. This is an example of being mentally relaxed enough to imagine being on a beach during the noon heat and allowing one's body to react as if the person was really there.

There may be a slight bobbing of the head or maybe even a spasm felt in the hands and feet. These movements, as with all of the other symptoms of hypnosis, will be slight in nature and usually only last for a short time. None of these sensations, however, will be felt once the person leaves hypnosis.

Most people report just a relaxed, almost sleepy feeling when they emerge from hypnosis, similar to just waking up from a nap.

The question is often asked during a lecture, demonstration, or other discussion on hypnosis as to whether the hypnotist can tell if someone is in the hypnosis state. The answer to that is that the hypnotist is never really sure, because a person can fake being in a state of relaxation and entering a daydream state. All that is really necessary to do so is to read a book or two on hypnosis and perhaps watch some hypnosis sessions to mimic the responses given by a subject during hypnosis.

Because hypnosis is very personal, all of it takes place internally and the hypnotist cannot enter a subject's thoughts and mind to see if he is achieving hypnosis or faking it. There are, however, some physical traits exhibited by a person in hypnosis, and there are a few simple tests the hypnotist can use to determine whether a subject is relaxed or not. Aside from these indicators, the hypnotist must rely on the subject's willingness to go into hypnosis. After all, without the cooperation of the subject, the session is doomed to failure from the beginning.

Some of these indicators I have already touched on, such as the abdominal breathing. A subject breathing slowly and evenly is a good indication that he is relaxing and responding to the suggestions being offered. This slow breathing pattern is not easily held by someone trying to trick the hypnotist; after awhile, normal breathing will return.

During the induction phase of the session, I want to see noticeable signs that the body is relaxing. When the shoulders drop and any signs of movement cease, this usually indicates to me that the subject is beginning to go into hypnosis. That is when I pay attention to the neck and head. When most individuals, myself included, relax and allow themselves to go into hypnosis, the head drifts off to one side or the other as the neck relaxes (see Figure 5.1). While this position may seem to be awkward and uncomfortable, it is not perceived as such by subjects in hypnosis and in fact appears to be quite comfortable for them. This particular cue, the head and neck position, is a sign to me that the subject is accepting my suggestions and is allowing himself to be hypnotized.

Another thing the hypnotist watches is the eyes. Rapid eye movement (REM) is a good indication of the presence of hypnosis. The eyes move back and forth — under the lids — as a scene comes into play in the mind. REM takes place only when we are dreaming or under hypnosis. Another way in which the eyes tell the hypnotist he is on the right track is how the eyes move when the subject is asked a question. If they move as a result of a stimulus suggested by the hypnotist and the movement is natural, then the client is probably in hypnosis.

Following are some examples of eye movement (remember that these can occur with the eyes open or closed). If the eyes move upward and to the right, then the client may be trying to envision a scene he has never seen before — such as when the hypnotist asks a subject who has never been to

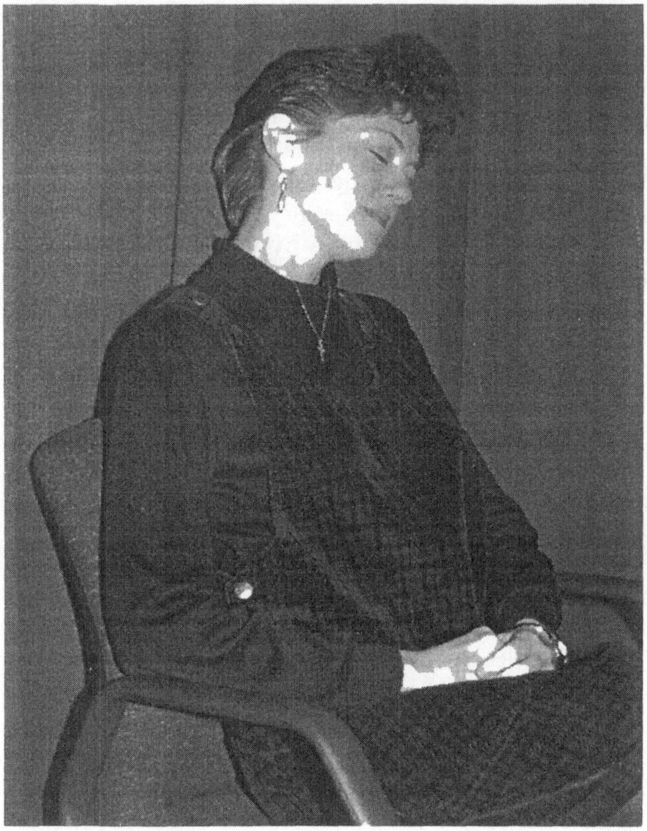

**Figure 5.1** During hypnosis, the head often drifts to one side. Although this may look uncomfortable, the subject feels quite relaxed.

a beach to take a stroll along a beach. In this case, the creative part of the mind will have to conjure an imaginary scene, and the eyes may move upward and right — toward the creative portion of the brain — to "see" it.

On the other hand, if the eyes move upward and to the left, the mind is seeing a familiar scene. This movement is toward the area of the brain where memories are stored. After being given a stimulus from the hypnotist, the subject's eyes may go in this direction, which is a good indicator the subject is remembering the past. This information can be useful to a hypnotist, because it can be used to the subject's benefit.

These are just a few examples to assist you in determining whether or not a subject has gone into hypnosis. There are other eye indicators (i.e., looking level and to the left could indicate a remembered sound), but you do not want to get so involved with trying to determine whether or not the subject is in hypnosis that you forget the reason for the hypnosis.

A

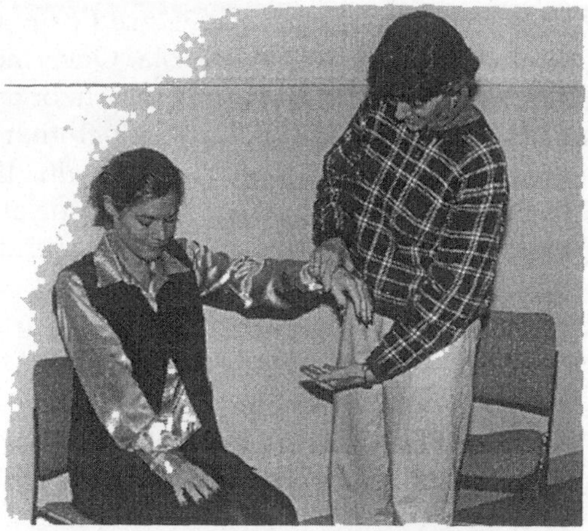

B

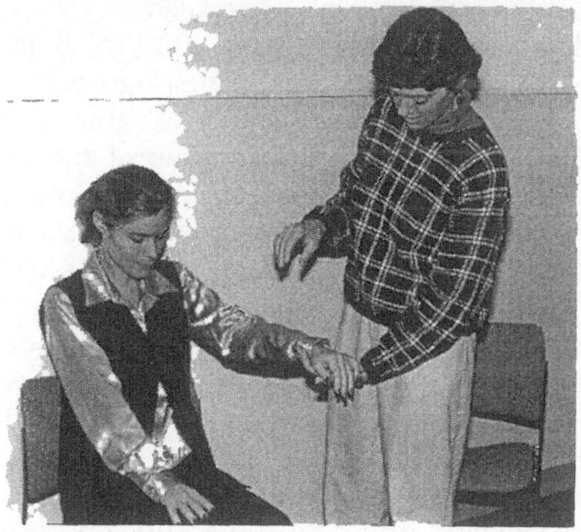

**Figure 5.2** To test for hypnosis, raise the subject's arm by holding the wrist and moving it slightly off center (A), then let go of the wrist and let it drop to the waiting hand below (B).

Here is a test, though, that a hypnotist can perform to determine if the subject is in hypnosis (see Figure 5.2). Have the subject sit with his hands in his lap. Tell him you are going to pick up one of his arms at the wrist. Then, raise the arm a short distance away from the lap but off to the side just a little so it will not fall directly back into the lap. Place your other hand directly below it so you can catch the wrist. When you are ready, let go and watch the reaction. If the arm limply falls into your waiting hand, then you can be fairly certain the person is very relaxed and in hypnosis. If, on the other hand, the subject directs his arm back toward his lap, you can be fairly certain that they are not in hypnosis and are resisting for whatever reason.

Another test is a little more drastic and is used primarily by physicians when they are using hypnosis as an anesthesia. Once the subject is placed into hypnosis, offer the suggestion that part of his arm or hand no longer feels any pain. After the suggestion has been given, pinch that part of the arm or hand where you suggested there would be no pain. If the person is in hypnosis, they will feel only a slight pressure or nothing at all. But, if they are not in hypnosis, then they will feel the pain and, depending on how much pressure you use, may open their eyes immediately. It is not so important, however, that the hypnotist detect whether or not a particular subject is in hypnosis, because ultimately it is the choice of the subject to go or not go. The hypnotist is only the guide who can help show the way.

Another concern that often emerges during a discussion on hypnosis is how deep into hypnosis a person has gone. The forensic hypnotist needs only a light level of hypnosis for a subject to retrieve details of an event, while physicians will often need to take their subjects into a much deeper state so that therapy or an operation can be performed.

One method of determining how deep into the hypnotic state a person has gone is to use Arons' master depth rule (Figure 5.3). The creator of the rule was Harry Arons, who was a founding father of the Association to Advance Ethical Hypnosis and has been one of the pioneers in America trying to bring respectability and professionalism to hypnosis. The Arons' method of instruction is one that emphasizes the scientific approach and drops the entertainment and mystical aspects often associated with the topic. He started a certification program that remains one of the most rigorous to pass even by today's standards. Part of his efforts included a depth gauge to determine the level of hypnosis of a subject. Familiarity with this depth scale is still required during the questioning part of the certification test for the AAEH.

The levels are broken down into six sections, with each section representing a different level of hypnosis and abilities portrayed by individuals who have experienced hypnosis. The following is a brief explanation of each level.

- Level 1. In the first level, subjects will experience many of the things already discussed in this book. They will feel relaxed, even lethargic. The body will appear calm with abdominal breathing. They will not be able to open their eyes if they are told they cannot. This is often called eye catalepsy.
- Level 2. As subjects slip deeper into hypnosis, they find that they cannot move isolated muscle groups, such as their arms or legs, if they are told they cannot by the hypnotist. Here also is where a person will begin to feel the heaviness or floating feelings discussed earlier in this chapter.
- Level 3. When subjects reach this level of hypnosis, they will begin to feel a rapport with the hypnotist, something the stage hypnotist is

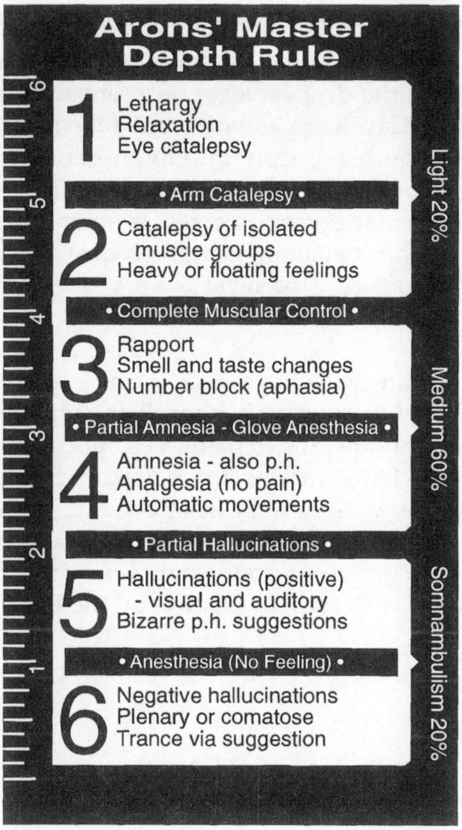


**Figure 5.3** Aron's master depth rule, used to determine the extent to which a subject is hypnotized.

counting on because it is at this level that a person can be told that he will not be able to say the number between 8 and 10 and when asked to count from one to ten will pass over 9 completely. The senses can begin to be influenced at this level, as well, especially the sense of smell.

- Level 4. Here a subject's perception of pain can be influenced, and the experience known as analgesia can occur. This is where pain is removed, such as for an operation or dental work. The subject will still feel pressure, but the pain itself will not be felt.
- Level 5. At this level, a subject given the suggestion that he has no pain will not experience any. A patient can be operated on while they are awake and feel nothing, just as if they were under regular anesthesia. A subject at this level can also experience positive hallucinations, both visual and auditory. This is where a person can be told there is a particular object in the room with him and he will see it, even though

it is not really there. A person will also hear a sound around him that is not really present, if he has been told by the hypnotist that it is there.

- Level 6. Here at the deepest level of hypnosis is the somnambulistic stage often portrayed on movies and television. The person is so deeply relaxed and so deeply into hypnosis that when he opens his eyes he can experience negative hallucinations, such as when he is told that a particular person or object is *not* in the room (even though that person or object actually *is* in the room) and he is not able to see that person or object. This level is very deep, and not everyone is capable of reaching this depth.

One person who can reach Level 6 on a consistent basis is hypno-artist Curtis Watkins. Mr. Watkins places himself into hypnosis, goes into this somnambulistic state, and begins to paint. His subconscious mind begins to take over to the point where Watkins, upon waking from his trance, does not remember painting the work now in front of him. The ability to reach this level, as I mentioned, is not common, but those who are able to reach it do such amazing things that one can understand how a person who reaches this level becomes fodder for the myths created by the entertainment media.

# chapter six

# A hypnosis session

By now, you should have a better understanding of what hypnosis is and the feelings that may take place when a person is under hypnosis. Perhaps the best way to fully understand is to be hypnotized yourself. For this exercise, you will need a tape recorder so you can record the following induction technique. Read through this chapter first so you get an idea of what an induction is like. Then read the hypnosis session into a tape recorder. When that is completed, find a comfortable chair and replay the tape. You will then be both the hypnotist and the subject. By doing this exercise, you will be able to gain a better understanding of what each person experiences during the session.

Before going into a full induction technique, I suggest using a shorter version. Many people are apprehensive about hypnosis because of all the misconceptions that have been passed down through the generations. To ease this fear or nervousness, the hypnotist must take the time to dispel these myths. In this book, up to this point, that has been attempted. There may still be some questions or some concerns that have not been addressed. Because of that, it is suggested that you read through this chapter and try the "self-talk" before trying the hypnosis induction technique. As was mentioned earlier, there is no harm that can come from hypnosis.

One warning should be given at this time — never use hypnosis or try self-hypnosis while you are driving a motor vehicle or operating machinery of any kind. The reason for this is when you are performing these tasks you need to be alert. Hypnosis is meant to relax you and take you close to sleep. No one wants a driver who is almost asleep behind the wheel of a car.

With that understood, try the following "self-talk" with a recorder first. This material was obtained at a hypnosis seminar in Ohio, but the author is unknown. The first paragraph is from the original version, while the second paragraph has been added by this author. As you speak the words, talk slowly and calmly. Pause in the breaks and do not rush the words.

"Take a deep breath ... breathe out slowly ... feeling all the tensions leaving ... taking another deep breath ... breathing out slowly ... feeling more at ease ... calm ... good to be alive ... peaceful ... lots of time ... more and more comfortable ... relaxed ... mind is clear ... calm ... open ... like a smooth lake ... flowing ... ready to enjoy new things ... fully alive ... replenished ... feeling very good ... .

"Take another deep breath, and let it out slowly. ... Take another deep breath. Let it out slowly, and as you do, open your eyes. ... You will be fully alert ... fully alive ... ready to reach new goals ... ."

Even with just this short "self-talk", many of the feelings associated with hypnosis that have already been discussed can be experienced; however, *not* experiencing any of these feelings is not unusual. Remember, each of us reacts in different ways. Many people who have used this "self-talk" have found that they become more relaxed, images of water (such as a lake or stream) come into their mind, and they have a general feeling of well-being. Some find that after this short experience many of their concerns about hypnosis have lessened.

Let's move on and discuss an actual hypnosis session. The session begins from the moment the hypnotist meets with his subject. The hypnotist must gain the confidence and trust of the subject right from the start, especially if they have never met before. Every effort must be made to display a professional appearance and attitude. The hypnotist must be calm, not rushed, and patient. All of these things will help a subject relax and trust the hypnotist.

Once the interview is completed it will be time for the induction technique. When you read the following technique into the tape recorder read it slowly and pause where the dots indicate to do so. When you perform this yourself, try to establish a rhythm known as "patter". Your patter will act as the background to help relax the subject so they can ease into hypnosis.

Sit in a comfortable chair. Do not cross your legs or arms; instead, place your hands in your lap. Sit with your back straight. Once you are in this position, you are ready to begin the hypnosis session. The reason you do not want your arms or legs crossed is that after a time those limbs will need to be moved. An uncomfortable feeling in your limbs will draw your attention away from the hypnosis process. Remember, we are trying to relax you, so make yourself comfortable.

[Begin recording here.]

"Take three deep breaths, letting each one out slowly. As you reach the third breath close your eyes, and just relax ... relax now ... concentrate all of your thoughts on my voice and relaxing all of your body ... relax ... feel the sensation of relaxation and release all of your tensions ... as you continue to breathe deeply with each breath you will find yourself slipping further and further into relaxation ... relax now ... I want you to concentrate on each part of your body. As I mention it I want you to release all the tension out of it and leave it in a peaceful, relaxed state. ... Let's start with your toes, and just release the tension in each one of them ... feel it leave your toes as you replace it with relaxation ... as you continue to breathe, with each breath you relax more and more. ... Now the relaxation spreads from your toes to your foot, the instep, to the heel, top and bottom, all the tension released ... your feet feel so good ... so relaxed ... so peaceful ... as you drift further and further, more and more relaxed. ... Now the relaxation spreads up your ankles ... pushing all of the tension and replacing it with relaxation ... more and more relaxed, confident and secure. ... The relaxation spreads up your legs to the calves ... more and more relaxed ... all the tension of the day passing by as you drift further and further ... confident and secure. ... The relaxation moves up to your knees, the front and the back ... and it feels so good to take the pressure off those knees ... so relaxed, so comfortable ... more and more relaxed. ... The relaxation now spreads to your thighs to your buttocks ... more and more relaxed ... peaceful and calm ... confident and secure in knowing you are in control ... all the tension being pushed from your body, leaving behind peaceful, relaxing hypnosis. ... The relaxation spreads across your pelvic area ... with each passing breath, you relax more and more. ... The relaxation spreads across your stomach to your chest ... very calm, peaceful, relaxed ... all the tension leaving your body ... euphoria spreads. ... The relaxation spreads up your spine to your shoulders ... it feels so good to relieve the tension in the shoulders ... very relaxed, very calm, peaceful ... like a nice massage, releasing the muscles, relaxing them, easing them ... more and more relaxed ... peaceful and calm. ... And now the relaxation spreads down your arms ... down the biceps and triceps ... easing all the tension out of your elbows ... so relaxed, so calm, so peaceful. ... The relaxation continues to move down your forearms to your wrists ...

more and more relaxed, peaceful, calm ... the relaxation moves to your hands, to the fingers. ... All the tension in your body flows out the ends of your fingers, leaving behind restful, relaxation. ... Each breath relaxes you more and more. ... Now it spreads to your neck, and it feels so good to ease the tension in your neck ... more and more relaxed ... confident and secure ... deeper and deeper into restful peaceful hypnosis you go. ... The relaxation spreads to your head, across your scalp to your forehead ... very comfortable, very relaxed. ... Now it spreads across your cheeks to your jaw ... allow your tongue to rest against the palate of your mouth and if your teeth are clenched, relax them. ... So now from the tip of your toes to the top of your head, very relaxed, very calm, more relaxed than you've been in a long time.

"While you are in this relaxed state I want you to imagine or visualize all the things I'm about to say. I want you to see in front of you an escalator, one like you've seen many times before ... there's the black handrail that moves in an endless loop ... the steps that appear beneath your feet and carry you effortlessly down ... the metal plate you stand on just before entering the escalator ... the shiny, almost mirror-like sides. This escalator has five floors. As we start down each floor, you will find yourself drifting deeper and deeper, more and more relaxed. It is a well-lit escalator. Plenty of light to allow you to see and feel comfortable and safe. And now we step on at floor 5 and we begin our descent. More and more relaxed ... comfortable and secure ... knowing that you are in control ... deeper and deeper ... you continue down the escalator, drifting deeper and deeper still. ... We come to floor 4 and you relax even more ... deeper and deeper ... more and more relaxed ... confident and secure. ... If you hear other sounds, simply acknowledge they are there and return to the escalator, finding that these sounds relax you even more ... more and more relaxed ... deeper and deeper ... you continue down and reach floor 3 ... more and more relaxed ... confident and secure you drift deeper and deeper ... feeling more relaxed than you have in a long, long time ... so peaceful ... so calm ... so relaxed. ... You continue to go deeper and deeper as you approach floor 2 ... you relax more and more ...

> deeper and deeper still ... confident and secure ... as you drift deeper and deeper you can start to see the bottom of the escalator, floor 1. ... The floor is well lighted and a comfortable setting awaits you as you drift deeper and deeper ... more and more relaxed ... you continue down until we reach floor 1. ... You step off the escalator and feel the thick plush carpet, the extra thick pad that cushions your every move. ... In front of you is a set of steel doors ... you are drawn to the doors and with a single move grip the door and open it ... you are basked in bright light as your eyes adjust to this new setting ... and you find yourself in your favorite place to go when you want to relax. ... This is the place you feel most secure, most protected, most relaxed ... and so you enter this place and feel more relaxed than you have ever been before. [Pause here for a moment to allow the subject to enjoy the feeling before going forward.]
>
> "And now it is time to come back. Back to where you are now, away from this peaceful place, your safe haven. ... You leave with the knowledge you can return here anytime you desire ... anytime you think about it. ... I am going to count to 5 and when I get to 5, I want you to take a deep breath, let it out slowly, and open your eyes ... 1, more and more awake, more and more aware ... 2, coming back to here and now ... 3 ... 4 ... and 5."
>
> [Stop the recording at this point.]

With this model of a hypnosis session you can see all the parts necessary for a successful session. First, there is the induction. In this example a general relaxation technique was used. This is by no means the only method of induction. There are many techniques, and the best technique changes from person to person. The induction is limited only by your imagination and that of your client (see Figure 6.1).

You may also notice there was no need for any objects such as a watch dangling on a chain. There are techniques that use objects for induction, but they are not mandatory. All you need to be able to do is create that daydream feeling, and the client will relax and slip into hypnosis.

One item that often enhances the success of a normal hypnosis session is background music. This music should be something soft and relaxing. There should be no singing, because this may distract the subject from hypnosis. Instrumental music is a good choice, as are tapes of ocean surf or a running

**Figure 6.1** Describing a quiet walk down a wooded path is one suggestion that can help the conscious mind slip into hypnosis.

stream or any other nature-style background noise. This may even help deepen the hypnosis, especially if you are, for example, having someone imagine himself on a beach. The sound of the surf and perhaps even sea gulls will help the person create the image more clearly in his mind.

Following the induction technique was the deepening section. In this example, escalator imagery was used. Just as for the induction stage, this part is limited only by your creativity. One item to note is that when you perform this part be sure to mention the fact that the area is well lighted and comfortable for them. The reason for this is that many people have fears — for example, going downstairs into a dark basement. If the technique you use reminds them of this fear it will prevent them from relaxing.

It is not always necessary to use a deepening technique. This is most helpful for first-time subjects, for individuals having a little trouble relaxing, and for other similar situations. It is recommended that until you and your subject develop a rapport where both of you understand there is no need for the deepening technique, you should continue to utilize one.

The last part of the session is when the subject is directed to a desired location. Once the person has reached this stage, the clinical hypnotist can offer positive post-hypnotic suggestions, and the forensic hypnotist can begin to ask for information about the crime under investigation.

Before moving on, there needs to be an understanding of post-hypnotic suggestions. A post-hypnotic suggestion must be something the conscious mind will accept. The conscious mind will not allow us to harm ourselves, so if we are given a suggestion to do something harmful we would open our eyes and come out of the trance. Remember the example where you are in the classroom drifting in the daydream state when suddenly the teacher calls your name? The same reaction would occur if the hypnotist were to suggest that you harm yourself or some other person. You would come out of the relaxed state.

Another less dramatic example would be a clinical session for weight loss. Some positive phrases the hypnotist could use would include "you take care of yourself and eat right" or "you like to exercise, and you feel energized and refreshed each time you exercise." These suggestions are positive and would be accepted by the conscious mind. Contrast these with a negative suggestion. Using the weight-loss example, a poor suggestion might be "you don't want to eat that fat greasy food" or "you don't like sweet food and won't eat fattening things."

The difference between these two examples should be clear to see. The positive example is more pleasing to hear. We are drawn to the words because they are encouraging. The negative phrase tends to put us off and keep us at a distance even though the words are meant to help us correct our habits. If these phrases can have such an impact *before* hypnosis, imagine the influence each would have while *in* hypnosis. This is why it is so important that the hypnotist know his client and understand the words to use to assist them reach their goal.

A post-hypnotic suggestion will only last between 24 to 72 hours. That may sound short when you compare this fact to the common misconceptions about post-hypnotic suggestions. Without the suggestion being reinforced on a regular basis, it will begin to dwindle in our minds.

Think for a moment when someone gave you praise for something you did. How did that make you feel? Probably pretty good. You felt pride in what you had accomplished and were pleased that others had noticed and made a comment about it. How long did that good feeling last? A day? Week? Month? Year? In most situations, the good words someone else tells us stay with us for about 24 to 72 hours. We will remember the comment much longer, but the good feeling induced by the words lasts only a short time. This is the same as for a post-hypnotic suggestion. The effect of the positive words to help us correct a problem or improve ourselves only lasts a short time.

Post-hypnotic suggestions should always encourage and help others. If you provide someone with a post-hypnotic suggestion, it is your responsibility to ensure that it is phrased properly and positively. Some of you may have seen a stage hypnotist who calls a person up on the stage and removes some aspect of his memory — usually something simple, such as the number 7, for example. The hypnotist has the person count out loud, and each time he gets to 7 (or a number plus, minus, times, or divided by seven), the subject skips it. The hypnotist must remove this suggestion for lost memory before the person steps down off the stage. This is an area, though, where an ethical hypnotist will not tread. You never want to take away the memory of someone. This would generally be considered unethical and could wind you up on the end of a law suit.

Let me use an example to help illustrate this. The names of the participants in this have been changed because who they are is not the issue. The situation unfolded something like this. Two people returned from a hypnosis school where both learned how to use hypnosis. Let's call them Bob and Tom. Bob hypnotized Tom for practice, and they wanted to experiment with their new knowledge. While Tom was under hypnosis, Bob gave him the suggestion that in their room was a map, and this map had several colors on it. Bob told Tom that the color yellow would become so bright that it would bother Tom and would reach the point at which he could not stand it anymore Tom was then to stand up, go to the light switch, and turn off the lights. When he completed this, he was to walk down the hall. Then Bob made his mistake. He told Tom that he would not remember the suggestion. Bob took away knowledge. This worked, because Tom trusted Bob and the suggestion was phrased in a positive manner. Tom knew he was to forget the suggestion, because his conscious mind agreed to accept the suggestion, but then a problem developed.

Tom did exactly as he had been instructed. When he got down to the other end of the hall, though, he was confused and disoriented. Bob had to track him down. When he found Tom, he realized what a mistake he had made and removed the post-hypnotic suggestion. Tom is okay now, but it was Bob's responsibility as the hypnotist to protect his subject and he failed to do this when he took memory away. The result was his client was confused and disoriented. This is nothing to play with. Never, ever, remove knowledge from a subject. A hypnotist must be responsible for his or her actions, and the health of the client must always come first.

As was mentioned earlier, all hypnosis is self-hypnosis. The hypnotist has no power or control over anyone. The only thing the hypnotist has control over is the choice of words. With this sample hypnosis session you should have a better understanding of how hypnosis can be achieved with the aid of a hypnotist.

There is a way for someone to be the hypnotist and the subject without the aid of a tape-recorded session or a hypnotist. It's called self-hypnosis. There have been many books and audio tapes devoted to self-hypnosis. The process is quite simple but requires discipline and practice. Once mastered, a person can call upon his subconscious whenever he wants to, without the need for a hypnotist or a tape-recorded hypnosis session.

There are three steps to this process. Each step is designed to develop the concentration and skill levels necessary to produce self-hypnosis. The important thing to remember here is that there is no race to get to the final process.

Each of us develops at our own pace, and some may stay in one stage longer than others.

Read through all three steps before you begin. In this way you will be able to see where you are going and how each step dovetails into the next. The steps are as follows.

## *Self-hypnosis, step one*

Before you begin, you should mentally tell yourself that you are going to do self-hypnosis. By telling yourself this, you are setting the tone for the practice you are undertaking. In other steps this will allow you, in your mind, to cleanse your mind of the day's activity and prepare for your dual role of hypnotist and subject.

You may practice this step in any comfortable setting. This will be the only step you can practice just before you go to sleep in your bed. For the other steps, as well as this one, you will want to find a comfortable chair to sit in. Do not cross your arms or legs. Remember you do not want to draw attention away from your desired goal. Get into a comfortable position, then take three deep breaths and let the air out slowly. Allow a moment to pass between breaths, but not so much that you are making an effort to breathe. On the third breath close your eyes.

With your eyes closed you are now ready to count yourself into hypnosis. Here you are becoming not only the hypnotist but also the subject. Begin with the number 5 and count yourself down to the number 1. Allow several seconds to pass between the numbers before you continue on to the next one. When you get to the number 1, you need to have a simple one-line phrase to tell yourself. A good choice would be something similar to "self-hypnosis helps me reach my goals." Whatever the saying you choose to use, say it to yourself ten times. If it helps you to count on your fingers to keep track, do so by using your thumb to touch the fingers on each hand.

After you have repeated your phrase ten times, it is time to count yourself out. Begin with the number 1 and count upwards to number 5. You do not have to pause as long between numbers coming up as you do going down, but you still need to pause. When you reach the number 5, take a deep breath, let it out slowly, and open your eyes. If you are in bed, just take a deep breath, relax, and go to sleep.

Try this step for at least five times during a week. If you feel comfortable with this after 5 times, move on to step two. If not, then perform it for another week before moving on.

## *Self-hypnosis, step two*

For this step you will need to position yourself comfortably in a chair. The main reason for this is that it will be easy during the early stages of learning this step to drift off to sleep. Mentally prepare yourself by saying you are going to do your self-hypnosis. If it will help you to relax, you may have some soft background music playing. Try to make it music that does not have any words so you are not distracted by what is being said in the song. Tapes of sounds of nature, such as the ocean surf, streams, or thunderstorms, are quite effective as background "music".

Once you are prepared, count yourself in as you did in step one. Take three deep breaths and close your eyes on the third. Count from 5 to 1 slowly, allowing time to pass between each number.

When you reach this point, imagine yourself standing at a blackboard. In one hand, you have a piece of chalk and in the other an eraser. See yourself write on the blackboard the number 50. Then see yourself erase it. Then write the number 49 and erase it. Then 48, 47, 46 ... all the way to 0. If you should find that during this process your mind begins to drift and you start thinking of other things, do not panic; it is normal. Simply return to the blackboard and write the next number. This number sequence is helping you to establish two things. One is a time frame you will need for step three and the other is stronger concentration power.

When you reach 0, see yourself turn from the blackboard and say something to yourself. This should be a simple one-line phrase, such as "I feel confident" or "I like myself" or "I am so relaxed." Again, you can come up with one of your own or use one of these examples.

After you tell yourself this one simple phrase, it is time to count yourself out. Start with the number 1 and go to the number 5. When you get to 5, take a deep breath and open your eyes.

You should perform this step until you feel comfortable with it. This will take longer than step one, so if possible practice this every day. This counting from 50 to 0 is what is called your "time set". This time set is what you will use in the third step.

## *Self-hypnosis, step three*

For this step, prepare a 3 × 5 card with your suggestion. Remember to keep this suggestion a simple one-line phrase worded in a positive manner. Read the suggestion five times. When you get to the fifth time, take three deep breaths, let the air out slowly, and close your eyes. With your eyes closed, count yourself in as you did in the other two steps, going from 5 to 1. When you reach 1, allow your suggestion to fill your thoughts. When you have completed your time set, count yourself out going from 1 to 5. When you get to 5, take a deep breath, let it out slowly, and open your eyes.

## *Sample suggestions*

Many books written on hypnosis mention that the suggestions offered during hypnosis must be phrased positively and be simple. This sounds easy until it is time for the reader to create phrases on his own. Many of the books do not contain enough samples of these suggestions to help the reader. This chapter will close with an offering of some suggestions and the situations in which they might be used. These are offered as an aid to the beginner and as ideas for the more experienced hypnotist.

### *Confidence*

I am strong and determined. People like me.
I see my self-worth and I am confident.
I have insight and see others like me.
I feel confident. I *am* confident.
I have unlimited abilities.
I have inner strength, power, and pride.

### *Image*

I am a winner.
I am positive.
I succeed.
I am focused and determined.

### *Success*

I am a doer.
I am successful.
I am filled with confidence.
I have high goals and I achieve them easily.

### *Reading faster*

I read better, faster.
I concentrate, focus attention, and read fast.
I enjoy reading and learning fast.
I am a fast reader.

### *Studying*

I retain and recall information.
I am a good student.
I love to learn.
I am prepared mentally, physically, and emotionally.

### *Exercise*

I like being in shape.
I see energy and power radiating within me.

Fitness is fun.
I am good to myself.

### *Reducing stress*

I am a calm, relaxed person.
It is easy for me to relax.
I like myself and take care of me.
I let go of stress easily, quickly.

### *Restful sleep*

I have a feeling of well-being and mental calmness.
I relax quickly, easily.
I enjoy my dreams ... pleasant, happy, helpful dreams.
I flow easily into restful sleep.

### *Positive attitude*

I project strength.
I am a doer.
I think and feel positive.
I am in control.

### *Leadership*

I am impressive, enthusiastic.
I am a leader.
People listen to me.
I have many strengths and talents, and I am success oriented.

# chapter seven

# The dangers of hypnosis

Hypnosis is a tool which we can use to our benefit, and like many tools there are proper and improper uses of it. People frequently ask whether hypnosis poses any danger and if there is any truth to the stories that have been passed down through the ages. The answer is that there may be more danger from some of the myths surrounding hypnosis than from hypnosis itself.

Hypnosis in and of itself cannot harm a person. Because all hypnosis is basically self-hypnosis, we control it ourselves and decide what to do with it. As we are not inclined to hurt ourselves, any possible danger from hypnosis is unlikely. Add to this the fact that we pass through hypnosis twice a day, every day, all of our lives without harm. To the scientific mind, it would seem that no possible harm could come from such a natural tool that most of mankind can utilize.

Still, any tool can be used either to benefit us or to hurt us. Danger associated with hypnosis does not come from the tool itself, but rather the person who uses it. The true danger lies in unqualified therapy at the hands of an unethical hypnotist.

One danger can be attributed to a person who is trained in hypnosis but promotes himself as a hypnotherapist, even though he does not have the educational background necessary to perform therapy. The unsuspecting patient who finds this person is entrusting their care to a person who does not really have the knowledge to treat them. The patient suffers from the hypnotist's lack of competency and spends his money on questionable treatments. The net result of such a transaction, however, will most likely only be a financial loss, with no significant harm to the patient.

When a person who wants to lose weight seeks out a hypnotist without first contacting his physician, that hypnotist is exceeding the limits of his training and is taking the safety of the client into his own hands. As was mentioned in an earlier chapter, a person wanting to have a hypnotist help him with chronic pain, such as headaches, should first consult with a medical doctor. Consider, too, the example of a person who visits a hypnotist to treat his sexual dysfunction, hoping that the use of hypnosis will overcome his problem. If the hypnotist is not qualified to offer such therapy, the welfare of the client is not the hypnotist's top priority.

There is another danger associated with the hypnotherapist who *does* have the proper educational background but who uses hypnosis improperly. Now, I know up to this point it has been discussed that hypnosis is natural and cannot cause harm, and this is true. During the therapy session with a psychiatrist, psychologist, or therapist there develops a strong doctor-patient relationship. This trust is usually much stronger than for most hypnotist-patient relationships because of the greater amount of contact experienced in a doctor-patient type of setting. A strong rapport between a hypnotist and a subject, however, can develop during extended hypnosis sessions, sometimes to the point where the subject wants to please the hypnotist.

Let's take this a step further and see what kind of trouble can come from this kind of relationship. While under hypnosis, the subject is open to suggestions that are phrased in a positive manner and represent no danger to the subject. However, it has happened that patients being seen by a hypnotherapist for emotional problems have not been treated ethically. Therapists have been known to suggest that certain events happened in the patients' past which would explain their behavior today, a danger known as planting "false memories". For example, there have been numerous occasions where therapists have suggested to their clients that they were molested by their parents when they were children, and this molestation was the cause for their current behavioral problems. This type of abuse by the mental health specialists shows how a tool that is to be used with trust can end up harming the person it is meant to help.

How can hypnosis hurt when it is a natural phenomenon we control? The answer lies in the trust and rapport that develop between therapist and patient. This bond is so strong that suggestions offered by the therapist can be accepted and influence the way a person thinks if he wants it to. For an individual searching for an answer to a problem, this type of suggestion could be just what they were looking for, even if the events suggested by the therapist were not true.

A recent example of this type of abuse was distributed by the Associated Press on November 30, 1997, in an article about an incident in Combined Locks, Wisconsin. A woman filed a malpractice suit against her psychiatrist and won a $2.4-million settlement for his misuse of hypnosis. The woman went to the doctor because she was depressed and began treatments that lasted over 6 years. During this time, she was told she had 126 different personalities. The doctor planted these suggestions and other false memories that left the woman suicidal. Some of these false memories indicated that she had been raped and pushed into an open grave. To aid him in his work, the doctor also prescribed various drugs that affected her thought processes. Shortly after she stopped seeing the doctor, her mind began to clear and she realized what had happened to her.

This type of abuse certainly represents a danger of hypnosis. However, if you examine this incident closely, you will see that it was not hypnosis that created the danger but rather the authority figure who abused his patient's trust. A tool is only as useful as the person who is using it. The trust represented by a therapist/patient relationship is one that is strong and easily abused by unscrupulous individuals.

Another danger associated with hypnosis is when the hypnotist does not do a thorough enough interview of the subject to be hypnotized, or the subject misrepresents himself and the therapist finds that he is working with a person who suffers from mental illness or hysteria. Only a qualified person should utilize hypnosis with a patient of this sort, and the lay hypnotist should excuse himself from undertaking such a task. You should stay within the level of your expertise and only perform the type and style of hypnosis you are trained to do.

However, you may find yourself facing a situation where you were not aware of underlying medical problems. On the surface, a particular individual may seem fine and completely in control, but during the hypnosis session the subject displays some unusual behavior. Some examples of these reactions may be the bobbing of the head in a rhythm with none of the other extremities joining in. These motions can be circular, rocking, swaying, or jerky. There may also be exaggerated breathing, and possibly the hands and fingers will tremble or the knees will move back and forth in unison.

These are just a few examples of the varied types of behavior that may occur during a hypnosis session. The important thing is for the hypnotist to observe the subject and if there are any unusual body movements to take notice of them. In these types of cases, it is imperative after the session that the lay hypnotist refer the subject to a trained professional to seek help and guidance. The hypnotist who is not trained in these matters must not go any further with a client of this sort.

What if you are faced with such a situation? What course of action should be taken when a subject suddenly begins to display one of these or another reaction? The answer is to reach out and physically stop the reaction. For example, if the head is bobbing, simply hold the head for a moment to stop the movement and follow this up by suggesting that the subject go deeper into hypnosis. Then bring him out of it. Do not try to continue on with such a subject, because you have no idea what kind of therapy he is likely to need unless this is your specialty area. Once you bring the subject out of hypnosis, discuss his condition with him and strongly suggest that he seek out a qualified professional.

When this happens during a session it can be quite startling. On one such occasion, during the interview with a subject, there was no indication of any problem. I began the induction technique, which was a general relaxation technique. Shortly after I completed this phase of the hypnosis session, the subject began to jerk his head backwards. This was the first time something like that had happened to me, and I watched in amazement as the subject repeatedly took on the relaxed appearance of someone going into hypnosis, with his head drifting into a relaxed position, only to jerk his head back each time. I then realized what I was witnessing and stopped his head movement. I remembered my teachers telling me that if you have to stop the movement three times you need to bring the person out of hypnosis. I allowed this subject to repeat this reaction three times and did as I had been taught to bring him out of hypnosis.

I questioned my subject after the session and wanted to know what he saw or was thinking during the session. He told me that when he closed his eyes and started to relax he saw a huge hole in the floor directly in front of him and he kept pulling back from it. I referred the subject to seek out more professional help because this reaction might have been masking some kind of emotional or mental problem. But it was an excellent learning experience in that it is one thing to be told this may occur during a session but it is quite another to actually experience it during a session you are conducting.

Not so much a danger from hypnosis but a danger to the hypnotist comes from claims of sexual misconduct by the hypnotist. Because of the misconceptions of hypnosis, some hypnotists have found themselves wrongly accused of improper conduct with clients of the opposite sex during hypnosis sessions. Unfortunately, there have been claims that have been completely justified, and the unethical hypnotists have been brought up on charges. For the ethical hypnotist, however, false claims from a client can create many problems. Because of this, precautions should be taken during any kind of hypnosis session in which a member of the opposite sex is involved.

Having a witness present whenever possible might be a good idea as long as the witness is the same sex as the client. The client would have to find this person agreeable, or else the session will start out on the wrong foot. Another suggestion is to tape the entire session (audio or video) when working with a member of the opposite sex. The forensic hypnotist will have to do this as a rule anyway, but any other hypnotist can benefit from the security of having the session taped to be used to counter any improprieties that might subsequently be claimed. Some dangers are not really dangers, if a little thought and planning are applied With sophisticated equipment being developed every year, there are more options for the hypnotist to ensure their safety and that of their clients.

These are the only true dangers associated with hypnosis for both the client and the hypnotist. The danger to the client comes from unqualified therapy and improper use of trust on the part of a hypnotist. It does not come from hypnosis itself. False claims of misconduct represent a danger to the hypnotist. At the beginning of the chapter, I mentioned that there may be more danger created by the myths surrounding hypnosis than by hypnosis itself. Let's take a quick look again at a few of these myths to show them for what they are.

One of the concerns often expressed is the fear of being trapped in hypnosis. There have been stories passed down through the ages of people who were placed into hypnosis and were not able to emerge, even after the hypnotist has told them they could. You should see that there is more myth to this belief than truth. If a person were left alone after being hypnotized, he would either wake up or merely go to sleep. This would not take very long, and the subsequent sleep certainly would not turn into days. If a person does not come out of hypnosis after being told he can by the hypnotist, then he is remaining in hypnosis because he wants to. Remember, all hypnosis is self-hypnosis and once the hypnotist stops giving suggestions the subject is left on his own. It is the subject's choice to remain in the relaxed state.

While the fear of being trapped in hypnosis may not be considered a major fear or danger to some, there are those who believe the hypnotist holds some kind of power over his subjects. This fear is often behind the belief that if someone allows himself to be hypnotized then he is a weak-minded individual. There are many examples of movies and television shows where hypnosis has been used and a character, usually a member of the supporting cast, is easily hypnotized. This character is also usually a person who is not as smart as the other members of the show and his hypnosis usually adds to the comic effect. While this may enhance a show and be good entertainment, it also helps foster the idea that only those with low IQs allow themselves to be hypnotized.

Actually, the authors who wrote the scripts for those shows have it reversed. The more intelligent a person is, the easier it is for him to go into hypnosis. The explanation for this has to do with concentration and the ability of a person to hold a thought for a prolonged period of time. During a hypnosis session, the hypnotist will offer words and phrases which the subject will use to create images in his mind. The usual hypnosis session can last anywhere from 20 minutes to an hour, depending on what the session is for. It takes a person with a strong level of concentration to be able to hold these images for that long a period of time. Hypnosis is, after all, similar to a sustained daydream, and to hold such images takes a strong imagination. I have found that it has always been easier for me to hypnotize creative people such as artists or writers because their imaginations are so vivid and they are used to being creative with their thoughts. They are able to take the words I offer them and to hold the images they create for the entire length of the session.

Individuals with very low IQ levels or those who suffer from mental impairment or mental illness are not able to hold images based on words for a prolonged period of time. Because of this they become bored with the exercise and usually become distracted, which is not beneficial to a hypnosis session.

One of the reason children under the age of 5 cannot normally be hypnotized is for the same reason — they simply do not have the concentration power to maintain the image in their mind. Lacking this ability, they are not able to go into hypnosis, but as they grow and develop into teenagers quite the opposite happens. Teenagers, I have found, usually make good subjects for hypnosis because they are at an age where their imagination seems to be at its peak, and their levels of concentration are just as high. These two forces working together can make for an excellent hypnotic subject. During forensic hypnosis sessions, I have found that they can offer many details to a crime scene that might have gone unnoticed by others. As we age, our imagination sometimes fades or our powers of concentration diminish, and so too does our ability to maintain the images necessary for hypnosis.

There should be no shame or fear associated with the ability to go into hypnosis. Often during a lecture or demonstration on hypnosis a volunteer from the audience is requested to come up and experience hypnosis. This is usually met with looks of "please don't pick me" until one brave person stands and is willing to try it. The opposite usually happens at a hypnosis convention. When asking for volunteers, the demonstrator usually has to hold the willing participants back. One of the reasons for this is someone well-versed in hypnosis knows there is nothing to fear and no shame in being a willing participant to a hypnosis session.

In 1993, I gave a presentation on forensic hypnosis to the Malice Domestic Mystery Writers Conference in Washington, D.C., and was fascinated at the reaction I received during the lecture. When I started the talk, there was plenty of movement and fidgeting in the seats. A low hum of voices could be heard, because while I spoke there were private conversations going on throughout the crowd. As part of my presentation, a well-known mystery writer agreed to let me do an induction on her in front of her colleagues. As I began the induction using a general relaxation technique, a hush fell over the large auditorium. The hush continued as I deepened the hypnosis, and I could look out at the faces and see several who were beginning to let their heads drop just as my volunteer's head was. Before I ended the session, I also noticed people beginning to shift in their seats as if fighting off the urge to relax. I ended the session and the room returned to its normal noise level. What fascinated me about this incident was how captivated by the subject people became when they felt they were "safe" due to someone else being hypnotized. When they felt themselves experiencing undeniable effects from the suggestions being offered at the front of the room, there were those who had to fight these off as if they were bad. Could these individuals still be influenced by fiction writers who have misrepresented hypnosis now that they successfully resisted hypnosis? Perhaps, or perhaps they were resisting because they feared being made to do something like bark like a dog.

Mind control by the hypnotist has always been dependent upon this fear of hypnosis. When a person learns that I am a hypnotist, the reaction is sometimes quite humorous, as there are those who will not look me in the eye because they are afraid I will be able to cast a spell on them. There are others who will stand in front of me and wiggle their fingers like they are casting a spell. All of these reactions, while humorous, reveal a fear that people will not be able to control themselves against the hypnotist's power. By this point, though, you should understand that this is completely without basis in fact, and the hypnotist does not have the ability to control someone's mind, the exception being the discussion at the beginning of this chapter regarding the abuse of the therapist-patient relationship. No hypnotist can just walk up to someone on the street and stare them in the eyes to make him do his bidding. Think about it. If someone were to try that with you or anyone you know, would it work? It's doubtful, and, depending on the person, it will probably only result in laughter.

Another fear derives from religious beliefs. Without getting into a long discussion on all of the various religions throughout the world, it should be stressed here that hypnosis is not a religion. It has no dogma, no teachings, no philosophy. It is and always has been merely a tool that can be used for a variety of purposes. Hypnosis does not threaten any religious belief, because it does not teach anything; for the same reason, a hammer, saw, rake, or broom cannot threaten any belief, either.

While working with witnesses and hypnosis I have come across some individuals who had been told by their minister that they should not go under hypnosis because it is evil and it opens their mind up for evil things to happen to them. If someone believes this, then the hypnotist should respect this belief and not place any pressure on the person to undergo hypnosis. This goes back to the three elements necessary for a hypnosis session to take place — freedom from fear, willingness, and confidence in the hypnotist. If a potential subject is telling you that he does not think he should go under hypnosis because it will allow evil to enter his mind, then he is obviously afraid of hypnosis and will not want to do it, so already you have two of the elements missing for hypnosis to take place. And if a hypnotist persists in having the person go under hypnosis, then the third element will probably be lost as well.

If the subject is merely asking for further understanding of the subject, then it is permissible for the hypnotist to take the time to explain that hypnosis is just a tool. Only if the client is looking to make the decision for himself would I venture down this path. Religion is a very personal thing, and if someone believes that hypnosis is bad, then no discussion will persuade him otherwise. It is best to walk away from that session.

If a subject is seeking more information about hypnosis to make up his own mind, then I would explain much of Chapter 1 to him. I would also ask if he has any questions in an attempt to find out what his concerns or fears are so that I can address them.

On the topic of religion it could be offered that one of the most conservative churches in the world today is the Roman Catholic Church, which recognizes that hypnosis is a part of our own natural ability and not the work of the devil. It further sets down a code of ethics for the hypnotist and states that hypnosis is not to be used for an illicit end. Traditionally, the Roman Catholic Church has not taken a stand on an issue until it has done extensive research into the situation. These decisions are usually made after much thought and discussion has been carried out, as is the case with most churches.

Once the decision is made, the church stands on its decision for a long time. What may be of interest to some is that the Roman Catholic Church made its decision about hypnosis in 1847, and it has remained consistent ever since.

Many religions use hypnosis as part of their rituals, and this is how hypnosis has come to be confused with religion. Hypnosis is also used in various forms in other rituals, such as a vision quest of Native Americans. Such uses of hypnosis do not make hypnosis a religion any more than using a candle during a service makes the candle part of that religion.

The bottom line for the religious aspect, however, is that, if a subject believes that the use of hypnosis runs counter to his religious beliefs, then the hypnotist should accept this and look elsewhere to use their talents.

The use of hypnosis as a tool has been stressed here, and its use in that capacity offers many benefits and great potential which we are still discovering every day. It is not a toy and should not be played with by individuals who are not trained and experienced in it. Just as a tool used as a toy can have the potential for danger and to cause harm to others, so too can the misuse of hypnosis cause difficulties, especially when it is misused by a person of trust such as a therapist.

# chapter eight

# Common questions about hypnosis

## *Has hypnosis cured any illnesses?*

While hypnosis has been used to help physicians in many areas, hypnosis by itself *cures* nothing. The greatest benefits of hypnosis are found in the areas of relieving pain and summoning the body's own healing forces, and there has been some progress in using hypnosis to help cancer patients reduce their pain. Research is ongoing, but there still is much we do not know about the body's ability to fight disease and ways in which hypnosis can be of help in the battle.

## *Does everyone behave differently under hypnosis?*

Since we are all different — each with different skill levels, abilities, and personalities — we each react uniquely. Some people are more suggestible than others and so may benefit from hypnosis more than those who are not. Others may go into a deep trance-like state, while others hover in a very light stage of hypnosis. Creative people, such as artists, often make excellent subjects because they are so imaginative. On the other hand, individuals who are more analytical, such as engineers, have a more difficult time being hypnotized.

When someone is given a word that suggests a particular feeling or scene, an artistic imagination is able to complete the picture. The analytical mind, however, encounters difficulty painting its own picture because it desires more details and specifics to fill in the gaps left by the hypnotist. So, the answer to the question is that we all do react differently to hypnosis.

## *A hypnotist makes appearances at local motels and guarantees success in smoking cessation and weight loss. Is he legitimate?*

There are many hypnotists who travel the country and offer these "guaranteed" clinics. The important thing to remember, though, is that there are no guarantees in hypnosis. This is very important to keep in mind. Think for a moment. How can someone who has never met you, who has never discussed your smoking habit or weight problem with you, be able to guarantee success? This hypnotist has no basis on which to make such a claim. Look closely at what he is offering in this guarantee. Most of these hypnotists say that if their technique does not work then you can attend another session at no charge. In the end, though, customers still lose their money, as there are no refunds.

Think about all that you have read in the earlier chapters. You should have picked up on the fact by now that this hypnotist should not be offering such a service — he should not be addressing customers' weight problems when the customers have not seen a doctor to determine if the reason for their weight gain is perhaps medical.

As for curing a smoking habit, remember that smoking is just that — a habit — and habits usually take some time to break. One session with a hypnotist is no guarantee that a person will never smoke again. To stop smoking, the person really has to want to quit, and the hypnotist cannot impose his will on the smoker to make him stop. Remember that the post-hypnotic suggestions he gives will only last for 24 to 72 hours. Odds are that shortly after the session the subject will still want to smoke and most likely will.

The only way to break a habit is to have the desire to do so within yourself. The hypnotist is there to give you some support, but sessions should be followed up with learning self-hypnosis techniques and moving forward. No one but you can guarantee your success. Traveling hypnotists make a lot of money, mostly because people are looking for an outside force to change their lifestyles. The truth is there is no easy road. It takes desire and work on your part to effect a change.

## *Will I be able to drive after hypnosis?*

Yes, you can drive after being hypnotized. Do you have any problem sleeping at night and getting up the next day? Of course not. Hypnosis is a natural part of our lives, but there still are some concerns about it. I have heard stories about people who have attended hypnosis classes and then been involved in car accidents on their way home. Later, these students have sued the school because they had been hypnotized and felt this was the cause for the accident. In all probability they were simply looking for a scapegoat. If you hear stories like this, use reason when evaluating them. There is a propensity for individuals to blame others for their own actions. Ducking responsibility for what we do appears to be an easy way out of trouble and, maybe, into some money.

## *What about all this "past life regression"? Is it real?*

This topic seems to be the most talked about in the hypnosis community. There is great interest in going back to another time. Part of this craze can be attributed to the media. Television and movie actors and actresses have gone on national television and claimed they have lived before. This type of media attention creates a ground-swell among the general population.

Some hypnotists are taking advantage of this interest. They claim to be able to take people back to another lifetime so they can heal what is wrong with them in *this* lifetime. This application of hypnosis threatens to drive the process back into the mystical world and out of scientific reasoning.

The basis for past-life therapy is a belief in reincarnation, so, if someone does not believe in reincarnation, there already is an immediate conflict with his beliefs. For this regression to work, just as for any type of hypnosis to work, all three critical elements must be present: freedom from fear, willingness, and confidence in the hypnotist. The last requirement is quite important for past-life regression. During the session, the client must feel a strong rapport with the hypnotist, which can lead to a desire by the client to please the hypnotist by doing what is asked of him to the best of his ability.

The hypnotist will give the client a suggestion about a past life. The hypnotist will offer dialogue such as, "If there are any images of past lives, let them come forward now. You will be able to speak and communicate with me."

At this point the client may pick up on images of another lifetime. Why? Remember that, during hypnosis, the subconscious is open to suggestion. The hypnotist, whom the client trusts and with whom the client has a strong rapport, has given the suggestion that something from the past will come to them. The power of suggestion during hypnosis is extremely strong. After all, that is what makes the post-hypnotic suggestion so effective — the power of suggestion.

The client may then begin to talk about things from another lifetime. People and places are described, as well as events. Again, though, let's think through this scientifically.

Do we not read and learn plenty about the past while we are going to school? Do we not see movies and television shows about the past? Most importantly, is the brain not capable of creating great entertainment itself? We dream every night. Are our dreams about things that actually happened? Or are they mere fabrications of the brain? There is a good probability these past lives are more a result of imagination than reality.

A competent, ethical hypnotist will not do past-life regression. Such a session, in short, could cause more harm than good. Aside from the possible confusion it could raise in a religious person, the benefits are negligible. There is no way to verify that someone did, in fact, live before. Without being able to check this out, too much doubt remains. There are those who will say that the past life they saw seemed so real. But have you not had a dream that, upon awakening, appeared to be as real as anything? The mind is a powerful tool. At times it can even make dreams seem real. Also, keep in mind that you can lie while under hypnosis. The "past life" could be based upon a movie you saw as a small child or a dream you had many years ago. It could be created from, well, just about anything.

Before running off to a hypnotist to see who you were in another life, consider that it might be better to live the life you have right now. After all. one life can have a lot happen during it.

## What is meant by "rapport" during hypnosis?

In hypnosis, it is desirable for the subject and the hypnotist to have a strong bond between them. This is developed as the two get to know one another and trust each other. This relationship sometimes get to the point that while under hypnosis the subject desires to please the hypnotist and therefore is willing to accept the suggestions that are made by the hypnotist. If this rapport is lost, then the subject will stop progressing because he will no longer accept the suggestions of the hypnotist. Confidence is an important element for rapport to take place. If the subject has confidence in the hypnotist, then there will be a high degree of trust. That is why it is extremely important for the hypnotist to behave in a professional manner and to nurture this feeling of confidence.

## What are hypno-aids and are there any advantages to using them?

Hypno-aids are various devices that can be used by the hypnotist during the induction of a subject. There are no magic powers in these devices; rather, they are things that the conscious mind can dwell on to enable the subconscious mind to open up for suggestions and to go into hypnosis. In short, they assist in the induction of the subject. There are many examples of these, such as the spiral, hypno-discs, pen lights, a watch on a chain, and many others. There is no need to use these unless the subject desires them. If a person is convinced that the only way he can go into hypnosis is with the use of one of these hypno-aids, then they should be used. Often people have been conditioned through various sources to believe that this is what a hypnotist must do to get people into hypnosis. If that is what the subject wants, using them will make the induction go more smoothly because that part of his expectations has been met.

## What is somnambulism?

Somnambulism is a very deep stage of hypnosis. Only about 20% of the population is capable of reaching this stage. An example of somnambulism can be found is sleepwalkers, who are capable of performing motor skills even though they are asleep. A person who is in a somnambulate state of hypnosis can do the same.

## What is the difference between analgesia and anesthesia?

Anesthesia allows a person to experience a loss of sensation with or without losing consciousness. This loss of sensation occurs throughout the body and is a total loss of feeling. Analgesia, on the other hand, permits a loss of sensation in a specific area of the body without the loss of consciousness. There is an insensibility to pain, but the person will still have a sense of touch or feel pressure. Both reduce or eliminate pain; however, there are differences in the extent of the pain relief. Analgesia is localized to a specific area and maintains a sense of touch, while anesthesia temporarily eliminates both the sense of touch and all other sensations.

## Can post-hypnotic suggestions become permanent?

Yes, they can, if the post-hypnotic suggestion is repeated many times over several sessions, either by self-hypnosis or with a hypnotist. There must also be a desire on the part of the subject for the suggestion to become permanent.

## What is "revivification"?

In hypnosis, this term refers to a subject who goes back in his life and relives an event. When this happens, often the emotions experienced at the time also return. This is a benefit for the forensic hypnotist, but not necessarily for the subject. When working with victims of crimes, in most cases they should not relive the event.

## What is meant by "abreaction"?

This is when a subject experiences an emotional release as a result of bringing to awareness something painful that had been forgotten or repressed. Abreaction also refers to abnormal reactions to hypnosis, such as rolling of the head or a jerking motion back and forth. In either case, the hypnotist is advised to bring the subject out of hypnosis and to refer them to a trained professional.

## *Are there any drugs that are effective in inducing deep hypnosis?*

Despite what has been written about them, there are no such drugs. Hypnosis must have an active, imaginative mind for it to work. The use of drugs will hinder the mind's ability to respond to the suggestions of the hypnotist, and the subject will not be able to hold the concentration level necessary for hypnosis to occur.

## *What is the difference between "auto-suggestion" and "self-hypnosis"?*

Auto-suggestion, the creation of Emile Coué, is a person repeating to himself a simple phrase over and over again each day. After some time has passed, the suggestion begins to take effect. One of Coué's most famous phrases is, "Every day in every way I am getting better and better." In self-hypnosis, the person places himself in a relaxed state and then offers a simple suggestion. If done consistently over time, this suggestion tends to realize itself.

The difference between the two should be fairly obvious. In auto-suggestion, there is no relaxing before the suggestion is given. Each day the person just repeats a positive phrase. In self-hypnosis, the subject slips into a relaxed state and then offers a suggestion. Both techniques are quite similar, though, and the phrases offered in both have the same positive, self-improvement style.

## *Is there a difference between hypnosis, meditation, and other Eastern teachings such as yoga?*

This is a good question, because there is some confusion regarding these techniques. Hypnosis is the directed use of our mental abilities which we use for a purpose, just as we would any other tool. One of the simplest was to differentiate between hypnosis and meditation, then, is to understand that meditation is the opening up of one's mind, blocking out all thoughts with no direction or control other than the goal of eliminating thoughts. Meditation is simply relaxing and clearing the mind. Hypnosis, on the other hand, is the result of a stimulus (coming either from the subject or a hypnotist) which has a direction and a purpose. This simple, fundamental difference should help you understand the difference and be able to explain it to someone who asks.

The second comparison is not so easy to clarify. Many of the Eastern teachings, such as yoga, karate, tai chi, and others, use a form of hypnosis during their classes. They can also utilize meditation. For example, a karate student trains very hard during the class. At the end of the class, the instructor tells the student to sit quietly and close his eyes. He then tells his pupil to imagine himself performing the techniques learned in the lesson that day and to picture himself in his mind's eye performing the technique perfectly. Sound familiar? While many of the Eastern-style teachings do not admit to using hypnosis, they often use similar imagery. As has been discussed, imagery, daydreaming, and the like are all forms of hypnosis; however, it should be stressed that hypnosis is not a *teaching*, Eastern or Western. It is a natural part of our bodies, a tool at our disposal to use and develop.

## *Is there a connection between hypnosis and the psychic sciences?*

Hypnosis has been lumped in with New Age thought and psychic phenomena on a regular basis. There are some unethical hypnotists who use this association to enhance their acts and increase the size of their incomes. The truth is, hypnosis has nothing to do with telepathy or clairvoyance. Since hypnosis is not a teaching, it cannot be considered a New Age philosophy. There is nothing to teach, except the mechanics of achieving the hypnotic state and using positive suggestion. Some New Age teachings make use of hypnosis, but one should not confuse the tool with the teaching. Hypnosis is rather like a computer; it can do what is asked of it but has no control over how it is used.

# *Part two*

# *Investigative forensic hypnosis*

# chapter nine

# Preparation for the forensic session

Understanding hypnosis and how to use this tool are only part of the total picture in regard to the forensic hypnotist. The primary difference between a forensic hypnotist and the others is that not only must forensic hypnotists follow established guidelines for hypnotists, but they must also be conscious of the legal system and what is permissible under the watchful eye of the courts.

When the forensic hypnotist receives a call from an investigator wanting assistance on a particular case, there are two points that must be made clear to the investigator right up front. The first is that hypnosis does not solve crimes. It is a tool, like any other tool, that the police have at their disposal, but by itself it cannot solve crimes any more than an interview with a witness can solve a crime. Information gained from a hypnosis session is similar to that obtained with an interview with a witness — the details still must be checked against the facts of the case and supported so that the information can stand up in court. The second point to be stressed is that hypnosis is not a miracle that can save a case by pulling critical information out of midair. Usually when an investigator comes to a forensic hypnotist, it is as a last-ditch effort when they have exhausted all other avenues and options.

Does this mean that hypnosis cannot help? No, and even a forensic hypnotist can be surprised by what comes out of a session. A jurisdiction neighboring my own department was working on a homicide case and wanted to see if one of their witnesses could remember something more to help them develop a suspect. I agreed to help them out, but when I was told that the homicide case was over 6 years old, I told the investigator that hypnosis was not a miracle worker but that I was willing to help anyway. We set up the session, but as I took the witness back in time I was very skeptical that we would obtain any details. The witness started to recount details. He worked at a bowling alley and was arriving for work. He remembered that it was raining that day and that there was an afternoon league so he had to park out away from his normal parking space. As he entered the lot, he glanced at the vehicles parked along the wall away from the bowling alley. When he walked into the bowling alley, he was approached by a woman who told him about a man bleeding out in the parking lot. The witness figured that it was probably a case of one of the workers at a local car manufacturing plant drinking a little too much and falling down, so he went out to investigate. As soon as he saw the pool of blood, he knew this was not just a drunk, and he asked another employee call the police.

It was interesting that a witness could recount so much 6 years later, but this information was already available from other witnesses, and nothing he had said up to this point shed new light on who the suspect in this case might be. The body was found next to a vacant parking space, while the victim's car was found in the next space with the car door still open. The detective handed me a note requesting that I find out what other cars were in the lot around the body. The witness described the vehicles going down the row until he reached another open parking space a short distance from a dumpster. I then had him compare this image with the one he had recalled earlier, when he was pulling into the parking lot. The witness remembered a Plymouth Duster being parked in the open spot. When we could not get any more descriptions of people or other details, I brought him out of hypnosis and we ended the session. Once the witness left the room, the detective was very excited, which I did not understand because I saw nothing in the details provided to warrant such a response. Then he told me that 6 years ago the suspect in the case drove a Plymouth Duster. Apparently sometimes hypnosis can come close to performing miracles. This case also showed me that the human mind is an amazing machine in that it can come up with such details after so much time had elapsed.

Having forewarned investigators not to plan on such miracles happening, the forensic hypnotist must now decide if a session can even take place, but there are some questions to be answered first by the investigator. Most important; is the person to be hypnotized a suspect in this case anyway? One of the rules for forensic hypnosis, as applied to law enforcement, is that suspects should not be hypnotized. The reason for this is that a person can lie under hypnosis. Remember back when I discussed the conscious mind and that it would not let you hurt yourself? The person who is lying to the police before hypnosis will not suddenly begin to tell the truth because they are now in hypnosis. He knows that if he did do the crime and confessed under hypnosis then the police would use that confession against him and prosecute. A person cannot be made to do something against his will, and a hypnotist cannot force someone tell the truth. Remember the three things you need to be hypnotized: freedom from fear, willingness, and confidence in the hypnotist. If the police are requesting that someone go under hypnosis in the hope that he will tell the truth and this person is, in fact, guilty of the crime, do you suppose he would be willing to be hypnotized? Would he not be afraid of telling the truth? This alone would usually be enough to keep anyone from going into hypnosis, so the session in all likelihood would be a failure and not result in a confession or insight into the crime. If anything, information from a suspect in a situation such as this would probably be an attempt to send the investigation in another direction.

Even though it was the defense that was instrumental in getting hypnosis accepted by the courts by having suspects hypnotized, the law enforcement community should steer clear of such a procedure. An example of the disastrous results of the police trying to use hypnosis as a truth detector can be found in an article published in the *Herald Journal* from Indianapolis, Indiana, in November 1989. The case involved a municipal department close to Indianapolis. The case occurred in 1982, when a woman claimed an intruder broke into her home and shot her two children. This same intruder then entered her room, knocked her unconscious, and left the residence. The woman described the suspect as wearing a Halloween mask, some coveralls, and a wig, but the children were unable to describe the assailant, because they had been sleeping when shot. Despite the woman's account of what happened, all the evidence in the case pointed to her being responsible for the shooting of her two children, including the fact that there were no signs of forced entry. This led investigators to believe that the suspect was a family member able to enter the home at will, which again indicated the mother. The police asked the woman to take a polygraph test, which turned out to be inconclusive. They then asked her to submit to a voice stress test, but the results were just as inconclusive as for the polygraph.

With no evidence directly linking the woman to the shooting, the police decided to have her go under hypnosis even though they knew that suspects should not be hypnotized. One of the investigators had attended a course on forensic hypnosis and remembered that suspects should not be hypnotized, but they proceeded with the session anyway. Under hypnosis, the woman described the suspect as her father, then she recanted this and said that it was an alter-ego of herself who had done the shooting. Without gaining any corroborative evidence, the police obtained a search warrant for her house using the statements made under hypnosis as justification and found a wig, coveralls, and Halloween mask that could have matched what the woman described the suspect as wearing the night of the shooting.

When the case went to court, it was revealed that the statements made by the woman were under hypnosis and that the prosecution had not been up front with this information. The result was that all evidence was ruled inadmissible, due to the hypnosis statement being the basis for everything. The charges were subsequently dropped.

This is why the police must not hypnotize suspects. There are other options. Not that I am attempting to second guess the investigators in this case, but perhaps performing a test on her hands on the night of the shooting to see if she fired a gun would have given them probable cause for a search warrant. They would have then found the items and, after questioning the suspect, come up with evidence that would stand up in court. It is the responsibility of the forensic hypnotist to make sure he is not endangering a case. The investigator is looking for ways to solve the case, and the forensic hypnotist must be able to determine if his expertise can help or not.

Once you have established with the investigator that the person to be hypnotized is not a suspect, it is recommended that you obtain only a little information about the case itself. This may seem to contradict what is true for most other types of police specialties, such as polygraphists, who usually want to receive an entire case file before administering the test. They do this so they can prepare their questions and have the information necessary to be able to go directly into an interrogation. The hypnotist cannot be afforded this luxury because of the very nature of hypnosis. Because suggestion is a major part of the hypnosis session, the hypnotist must be on guard not to make any kind of suggestions that would influence the person giving the information. To ensure that there are no preconceived ideas as to who the suspect is or what kind of information is needed, the hypnotist must be kept clear of the details until hearing them for the first time from the subject.

Knowing what kind of crime is being investigated, the date and time the offense occurred, and the location where it happened should be the extent of the forensic hypnotist's prior knowledge of the case. In the case of hypnosis, less is more when it comes to the outcome of a session. A hypnotist who is going in fresh with few details will be less likely to lead a witness or victim in the direction of a certain suspect. Because the hypnotist is hearing the information for the first time, he might have a new angle or perspective on the situation that could aid the investigator.

Knowing the date, time, and location will help the hypnotist prepare for the time regression necessary for a forensic session. During the session, the hypnotist will direct the witness or victim back to that particular place and time. Prior knowledge of the location can assist the hypnotist when he describes the setting to the subject. If the hypnotist is not familiar with the location, it might be helpful for him to look at the area before the session so he can help paint a clear mental image for the witness. Knowing the time of day is also important, as some landmarks may not be visible during the time the crime took place. The hypnotist should not assume anything about what the witness may have noticed, but being familiar with the circumstances helps to set the stage for exploring the subject's memory.

The date is important so that the hypnotist can direct the subject back to that particular time and day. There is no time limit on hypnosis, as demonstrated by the earlier example of the homicide outside of the bowling alley, but ideally the case should be less than a year old. Of course, a session should be held as soon as possible, especially when a composite drawing or other means of sketching suspects is to take place. The sooner this type of information can be distributed, the better, so ideally a session looking for this type of information should be scheduled as soon as possible.

That is the extent of the information the hypnotist needs to make a decision as to whether or not to do a session. The investigator may wish to present more of the case, but it is in the best interests of everyone involved that the hypnotist learn the facts of the case from the witness. There is less chance that the hypnotist can offer a suggestion that would taint the case, whether done intentionally or inadvertently.

Once the hypnotist agrees to perform the session, the next issue is the location for the session. The session should be held where there will be no possibility of interruption. A quiet location is preferred but not mandatory for hypnosis to take place. The preferred location would be at the requesting police department's location, for several reasons. The first is that this site is probably close to where the witness or victim lives and would be convenient for them. Another reason is that any information or evidence, such as the video or audio tapes of the session, can be quickly stored in the department's property room, keeping the chain of evidence intact.

If the requesting agency cannot accommodate the session, then the next most desirable location would be at the hypnotist's office or business location. This is primarily because equipment required for the session would be readily available. But having to choose between these two locations is not a hard and fast rule. The hypnotist and investigator should be flexible and willing to go wherever the witness desires. Remember, for hypnosis to occur, the subject must be able to relax. If the witness says that he cannot undergo hypnosis in a police department or office setting, then another mutually agreeable location should be picked.

In an internal theft case I worked on, the subject to be hypnotized was the last one who was in possession of some money that later came up missing. This employee was not suspected of the theft and so was not considered a suspect. The hypnosis session was to take place at her place of employment. I explained the process of hypnosis to her, and she said she had no problems with it and was willing to do it. However, she had difficulty relaxing and found she could not go into hypnosis. After some more discussion with her, I found that she was not able to relax because she was at work and felt uneasy about doing such a thing at her place of employment. We agreed to do the session at her house. The case investigator and I then went to her residence with all of our equipment and attempted the session again. This time, in her own home, she was able to go into hypnosis and was able to provide some in-depth details about the day the theft occurred and where the money was placed. The point here is that had we not been willing to move to her residence for the session, those details would still be held in her unconscious mind and would not have been available to help the investigator. So, while the location may seem like a simple item, it can mean the difference between success and failure.

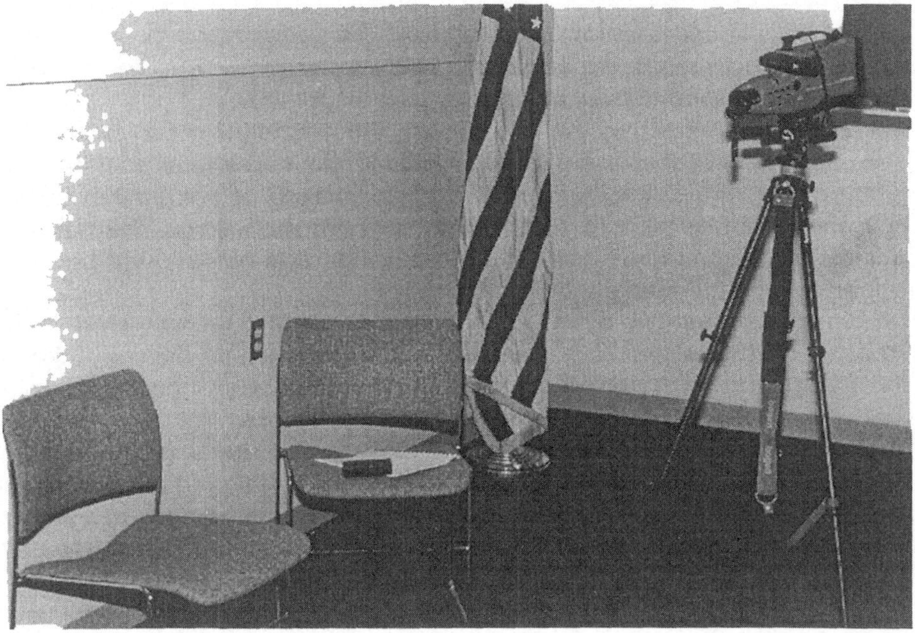

**Figure 9.1** The session room requirements are simple — a comfortable chair, recording equipment, and note pads.

The requirements for the room (see Figure 9.1) are minimal which should help in finding a suitable location. The room must be able to accommodate at least two chairs, one preferably padded such as an office chair or easy chair. The session may require a half hour to an hour, so the subject should be kept comfortable during this time. Any discomfort the subject might experience could shorten the session, as it becomes an irritant that draws attention away from the task at hand.

The room should also be large enough for the equipment necessary for the session. This, of course, depends on the type of session and if more specialists need to be present, but all sessions should be videotaped or at least audiotaped. The reason for this goes back to the power of suggestion. Since a hypnotist has the witness or victim in a relaxed state, there is the possibility that a suggestion could mislead or otherwise somehow direct the victim. The defense attorney will want to examine every word spoken during the session to make sure that this did not happen and that the session was performed appropriately. Also, by recording everything said during a session, the session can later be reviewed by the prosecutor, judge, and jury to determine if any of the testimony has been tainted by the hypnotist. The recording protects the hypnotist in that it can show that he did not lead the subject or offer some kind of suggestion.

Another reason for wanting the session videotaped is to record the physical actions of the hypnotist during the session. This protects the hypnotist against any kind of claims that he acted improperly, and it allows the court to observe the gestures and mannerisms of the hypnotist to ensure that no hand signs or non-verbal signals of any kind were offered to the subject. The session should be as sterile as possible, with the hypnotist merely being the facilitator.

When a video camera is set up to record a session, one must keep in mind that equipment does malfunction. There is only going to be one chance to record this session, which is why some kind of backup system should be in place. If such equipment is available, then two video cameras are recommended to record the session from two angles and to provide backup should one of the cameras malfunction. If such equipment is not available, then a simple tape recorder can provide an audio of the session and work as backup for the session. The quality of the recording equipment should be the best available. This is a one-time event that must be recorded There may be other times that this witness is hypnotized, but each session is different and must be documented. For example, in the internal theft case mentioned earlier, the first session with the witness was unsuccessful but that session was still recorded and kept. The second session was taped as well, because when a case like this goes to court both sessions will come into question and records of both sessions will be required.

The hypnotist will also need to take good notes during the session. This is done for a number of reasons, but primarily because there may be a time when both the primary and secondary recording devices malfunction and neither captures the session. The notes taken during the session will be the only record of that session. This was how sessions originally were conducted.

Also necessary for the session is having an accurate watch. Digital watches are perhaps the best for this, because they offer the time at a glance. During the hypnosis session, the hypnotist will need to document the time they begin certain phases of the session, such as the induction, but they will also record the beginning and ending times.

Other equipment that might be needed can sometimes be easily overlooked, but running down a checklist prior to the session may prevent problems. Included in this checklist would be extra supplies, such as pens or pencils and batteries for the video or audio recorder. Nothing is more frustrating during a session than to have a pen run out of ink or to break the lead in a pencil and have to scramble for something else to take notes with. This distraction impacts the hypnotist in that it may turn his attention away from the session. The same is true in regard to batteries. If the batteries suddenly run down, it is simple to pause while these are being changed, if extras are on hand. The important point to keep in mind when it comes to equipment is to have it available and ready to use. Remember that when the mechanics are working smoothly, the session itself has a better chance at success.

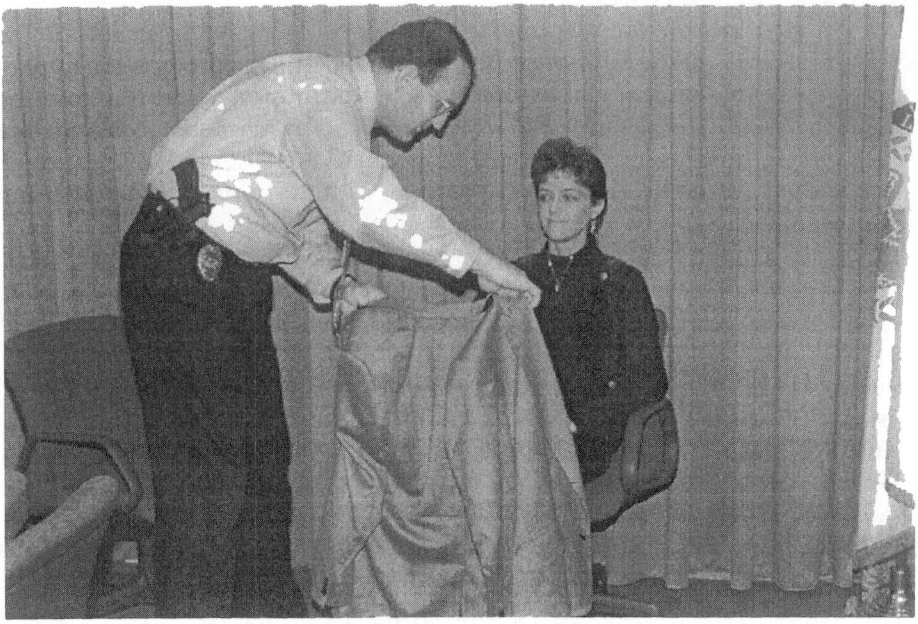

**Figure 9.2** A modesty shield can be anything from a blanket to a sport coat.

The only other items you may want to consider including in the session are tissues and a modesty shield. Because the witness or victim will be going back in time to view a crime scene, he may experience very strong emotions. Such strong feelings can cause the subject to cry. If the hypnotist has tissues readily available, it will save the subject some embarrassment, as well as providing some comfort by not forcing the subject to grope around looking for something to dry his eyes on. A modesty shield (Figures 9.2 and 9.3) can be anything to cover the legs and waist of a female subject. Because of the nature of hypnosis, there are some women who may feel vulnerable and uncomfortable about being in the situation. Placing a modesty shield, such as a blanket, across the subject's legs can alleviate some concern and provide a feeling of security. The feeling of being wrapped up in a blanket can often help relax a person and help to ease them into hypnosis. If a blanket is not available, then the hypnotist can offer his sport coat or that of the investigator to perform the same role. This simple item can make the session run more smoothly and provide that extra piece of comfort to make it more successful.

Having all of the necessary equipment available and having some information regarding the case in advance help the subject to reach hypnosis. The lack of certain items of equipment will not necessarily have detrimental effects on the outcome of a session, just as having all of these items cannot ensure a successful session. All the hypnotist can do is to provide a comfortable

**Figure 9.3** The modesty shield can provide an increased level of comfort.

atmosphere and present a professional image. The entire session hinges on the subject, not the hypnotist, and the hypnotist, investigator, and other interested parties must fully understand that.

# chapter ten

# Hypnosis and the courts

Can hypnosis be used in court? Many prosecutors will refer to their law books and reports to see if a witness whose memory has been refreshed can be used in a criminal proceeding. Courts in various parts of the country have each had differing views at one time or another; however, in 1987, the U.S. Supreme Court answered the question for all courts throughout the United States.

The Supreme Court concluded that lower courts could not completely ban the testimony of a witness whose memory had been refreshed by the use of hypnosis. The case leading to this decision was Rock v. Arkansas. The progression of this case was watched closely by many concerned with hypnosis. What is interesting is that the hypnosis session in this case was not performed by the prosecution. It was the defendant in the case who underwent the hypnosis. Justice Harry A. Blackmun wrote the majority opinion, and perhaps his words will shed more light here on this situation.*

> "We are not now prepared to endorse without qualifications the use of hypnosis as an investigative tool; scientific understanding of the phenomenon and of the means to control the effects of hypnosis is still in its infancy."

The high court added that, by a lower court refusing to admit the testimony of the defendant (Vickie L. Rock) in this trial, it violated the defendant's constitutional right to testify on her own behalf. Because of this, the defendant was able to testify even after undergoing hypnosis and having her memory refreshed.

The charge against Vickie Rock was one of manslaughter. She was accused of killing her husband in 1983. Mrs. Rock was not able to provide a very good description of the events that led up to the death of her husband.

* See Epstein, A., Hypnosis statements admissible, *Suggestion: The Journal of the Association to Advance Ethical Hypnosis*, 103, 21, 1987.

During the hypnosis session, Mrs. Rock was able to remember that the gun had gone off by accident. She had no intention of killing her husband. The gun was later inspected, was found to be defective, and could have gone off by accident.

Even though this case involved a defendant, the Supreme Court used it to put into place the ground rules for hypnosis. The testimony could be admitted into court, but any such testimony had to be backed up with evidence. Remember, anyone can lie under hypnosis, and for this reason it is recommended that only witnesses and victims be hypnotized. They have nothing to gain by being untruthful.

In writing his opinion, Justice Blackmun conceded that there are varied responses to hypnosis. Hypnosis cannot and does not guarantee accuracy; in fact, he noted that it often has no effect on memory whatever. Hypnosis serves merely to broaden both correct and incorrect recollections.*

So, when you are asked if hypnosis can be admitted into court, you can explain that, under Rock v Arkansas, the Supreme Court has ruled that its use cannot be ruled out. The justices will be closely watching cases that involve hypnosis, and as long as the hypnosis session is performed in a professional, ethical manner, such testimony should be able to be presented into the court proceedings.

Prior to the Rock case reaching the Supreme Court, other courts reviewed the hypnosis question. Their decisions still may have an impact on the role that hypnosis will be able to play in our judicial system. In July of 1981, four people were shot and killed in their own home. This vicious crime took place in Clermont County in Ohio. A daughter by another marriage of one of the victims was at the home the night before the murders. When police questioned her, she remembered seeing two other men at the home that night. One of these men was a business associate of her stepfather.

The police put together a photographic line-up made up of some of the known acquaintances of this business associate. The daughter was able to pick out one of the men and say that he resembled the man who was at the house that night. She added that there were something different about him, that his hair was longer than shown in the photograph. In an attempt to gather as much information as possible in the case, the daughter was hypnotized by an Ohio State Patrol officer who was trained in the use of hypnosis.

In a separate, but later related, incident in a small community in Ohio called Amelia, a police officer stopped a vehicle for a speeding violation. The officer did not issue a citation and gave the driver a warning without checking him through the computer or calling his traffic stop into the dispatcher. The officer did not think much of the stop until two handbags belonging to one of the murder victims were found shortly after the murders. When he was shown the same photographic line-up as that shown to the daughter, the

---

* See "Hypnosis Ban Upset by Court" in *Suggestion: The Journal of the Association to Advance Ethical Hypnosis*, 112, 14, 1989.

officer immediately identified the same person as being the man he stopped in his vehicle.

The same Ohio State Patrol officer who hypnotized the daughter was called in to hypnotize this police officer in an attempt to retrieve the license number, but he could not recall the number. Subsequent investigation revealed that the suspect did own the vehicle stopped by the officer that night. The defendant was convicted on four counts of aggravated murder. The trial court allowed the testimony of the officer and the daughter to be used in the trial, even though they had been hypnotized. The defendant appealed the case based on this refreshed testimony. The case was referred to the Ohio Supreme Court.

The Court reviewed the case and decided that the testimony had been admitted into court correctly. They went on to say that hypnosis was generally accepted in the scientific community as a method that can assist someone with their memory. However, the court added that the method by which the hypnosis was administered must come under scrutiny. It established some safeguards to ensure that hypnosis sessions do not influence the memories of the witnesses. They also made it clear that their views were not the final word on whether or not testimony would be admissible into court. Their findings were as follows:*

1. A psychiatrist or psychologist experienced in the use of hypnosis should conduct the hypnotic session.
2. The professional conducting the session should be independent of and not regularly employed by the prosecution, the defense, or investigators involved in the case. Nevertheless, the hypnotist may collect a fee from the party engaging his services.
3. All information given to the hypnotist must be recorded, either in writing or in another suitable form.
4. Before inducing hypnosis, the hypnotist should obtain a statement of facts from the subject as the subject remembers them.
5. All contacts between the hypnotist and the subject must be recorded.
6. Only the hypnotist and the subject should be present during all phases of the hypnotic session, including during pre-hypnotic interviews.

You may notice many of these same guidelines were already provided in an earlier chapter. You may also have noticed that this court recommended that only a psychiatrist or psychologist perform the hypnosis session, but this was a case in which the hypnotist was a police officer.

The justices did not mean to exclude individuals trained in hypnosis; they were trying to set a standard. They added to their decision that if a hypnotist has the proper qualifications and is competent in the use of

* See "The Court's Opinion on Hypnotically Refreshed Testimony" in *Suggestion: The Journal of the Association to Advance Ethical Hypnosis*, 101, 36, 1987.

hypnosis, then he should be able to perform the session whether or not he is a psychologist or psychiatrist. This is the door that has allowed non-medical personnel to be able to conduct forensic hypnosis. Since this decision was made in 1984, the field of hypnosis has opened up significantly and has gained more recognition by the medical and scientific community.

In 1987, the U.S. Supreme Court had another chance to look into the usefulness of hypnosis during a criminal investigation. Brett C. Kimberlin was convicted in 1980 of a speedway bombing spree in Indiana and for violating federal narcotics laws. He was serving a 50-year sentence for these violations when his appeal reached the high court.

Several witnesses were hypnotized and testified that they saw Kimberlin purchase materials similar to those used in the bombs planted in the speedway area. Kimberlin argued that a person who undergoes hypnosis is open to suggestions from the hypnotist. Because of this, Kimberlin wanted these witnesses' testimony removed from evidence and his conviction overturned. In a 5-4 vote, however, the Supreme Court upheld hypnosis testimony as being admissible in a court hearing. The justices again confirmed that if done properly, a person may have his memory refreshed by hypnosis, and this refreshed memory can be admitted into court.

This case, as was the one in Ohio, was a victory for the prosecution and for forensic hypnosis. In both of these cases, it was the witnesses who were placed under hypnosis. These people had no reason to lie and no vested interest in telling (or not telling) what they remembered. Because of this, their refreshed testimony can be accepted for what it is, as opposed to the case of a suspect given the opportunity to fabricate memories to help his case.

In 1988, a Federal judge in New York had the chance to decide if he would allow hypnosis-refreshed testimony. The case involved members of the Gambino organized crime family. These Gambino members were responsible for the abduction and murders of a dozen people. A witness to the abduction of a man name Andrei Katz (whose body was subsequently found dismembered) was placed under hypnosis by the police. The witness was able to provide information from her refreshed testimony that implicated members of the Gambino crime family in the murder of Mr. Katz. Judge Vincent L. Broderick decided that he would allow the testimony of the witness into the trial. He did this even though the defense claimed the police asked leading questions during the hypnosis session. This is why it is so important for you to document properly every word spoken to witnesses while they are under hypnosis. Audio and video tapes will give judges in the future the ability to examine the entire session and provide a clear picture of what went on during the session. Keeping the session admissible is the responsibility of the hypnotist.

These are only a few sample cases of how the courts are looking at hypnosis. You will need to inquire at your own prosecutor's office as to whether they see any problems in using hypnosis. The cases provided here should help you explain to them that the U.S. Supreme Court on two occasions had the chance to exclude hypnosis and on both occasions allowed the testimony to be used in the trial. Each state may view things differently as far as the guidelines they will accept for hypnosis-refreshed testimony; however, if you follow the guidelines listed earlier and limit your comments to appropriate terms and phrases, the testimony should be able to be admitted based on the Supreme Courts decision.

Refer to the following list for hypnosis-related cases:*

**U.S. Supreme Court**

Rock v. Arkansas 708 S.W. 2d 78 (Ark. 1986)

**Federal courts**

1st Circuit - Clay v. Vose, 771 F. 2d 1 (1st Cir. 1985)
2nd Circuit - U.S. v. Miller, 411 F.2d 825 (2nd Cir. 1969)
4th Circuit - Harker v. Maryland, CA4 (4th Cir. 1969)
5th Circuit - U.S. v. Valdez, 722 F. 2d 1196 (5th Cir. 1984)
5th Circuit - Wicker v. O.L. McCotter, 783 e. 2d 487 (5th Cir. 1986)
6th Circuit - Beck v. Norris, CA6 No. 85-6043 (6th Cir. 9/19/86)
8th Circuit - Spryncizntyk v. General Motors, No. 84-1566 and 84-1611 (8th Cir. 1985)
9th Circuit - U.S. Awkard, 597 F. 2nd 667 (9th Cir. 1979)

**State courts**

Alabama - Prewitt v. State, 460 so. 2d 2986 (Ala. Cr. App 1984)
Alaska - State v. Conteras, 647 P. 2d 792 (Alaska App. 1983)
Arizona - State exrel Collins v. Superior Court, 644 p. 2d 1296 (1982)
California - People v. Shirley, 641 P. 2d 775 (1982)
California - People v. Thompson, 176 Cal App.3d.554 (1986)
Colorado - People v. Quintanar, 659 P, 2d 710 (1982)
Connecticut - State v. Atwood, 479 A 2d 258 (Conn Sup 1984)
Delaware - Delaware v. Paul E. Davis, 490 A 2d 601(1985)
Florida - Bundy v. State, 471 So. 2d 9 (1985)
Georgia - Collier v. State, 261 S.E. 2d 364 (1979)
Georgia - Felker v. State, 314 S.E. 2d 621 (Ga. 1979)
Hawaii - State v. Moreno, 709 P. 2d 103 (Haw 1985)
Idaho - State v. Iwakiri, 682 P. 2d 571 (Id 1984)
Illinois - State v. Gibson, 4 App. 81CF 243 (1983)
Illinois - People v. Calhoon, 457 N.E. 2d 998 (Ill App. 1984)
Indiana - Pearson v. State, 441 N.E. 2d 468 (1982)
Indiana - Strong v. State, 435 N.E. 2d 969 (1982)
Indiana - Peterson v. State, 448 N.E. 2d 673 (1983)
Iowa - State v. Seager, 431 N.W. 2d 420 (1983)
Kansas - State v. Conley, 627 P. 2d 1174 (Kan App 1981)

* See Baranowski, G.H., Forensic hypnosis ... to be or not to be? What saith the laws of the land?, *Suggestion: The Journal of the Association to Advance Ethical Hypnosis*, 109, 11–12 and 23, 1989.

Louisiana - State v. Wren, 425 So. 2d 756 (1983)
Louisiana - State v. Goutro, 444 So. 2d 615 (1984)
Maryland - State v. Collins, 464 A 2d 1028 (Md App. 1983)
Massachusetts - Commonwealth v. Kater, 447 N.E. 2d 1190 (1983)
Michigan - People v. Nixon, 346 N.W. 2d 743 (1985)
Minnesota - State v. Ture, 353 N.W. 2d 502 (Minn App. 1984)
Minnesota - State v. Blanchard, 315 N.W. 2d 427 (1982)
Mississippi - House v. State, 445 So. 2d 815 (1982)
Missouri - State v. Little 674 S.W. 2d 541 (1984)
Nebraska - State v. Patterson, 331 N.W. 2d 500 (1983)
Nebraska - State v. Palmer, 313 N.W. 2d 648 (1981)
New Jersey - State v. Hurd, 432 A. 2d 86 (1981)
New Mexico - State v. Beachum, 643 P. 2d 246 (N.M. App 1982)
New York - People v. Hughes, 453 N.E. 2d 484 (N.Y. App. 1983)
North Carolina - State v. Payne, 325 S.E. 2d 205 (N.C. App 1983)
North Carolina - State v. Peoples, 299 S.E. 2d 205 (N.C.App. 1983)
North Dakota - State v. Brown, 337 N.W. 2d 138 (1983)
Ohio - State v. Weston, 475 N.W. 2d 138 (1983)
Ohio - State v. Maurer, 473 N.W. 2d 768 (Ohio 1984)
Oklahoma - Robinson v. State, 677 P. 2d 1080 (Okl Cr. App. 1984)
Oklahoma - State v. Luther, 663 P. 2d 1261 (1983)
Oregon - State v. Jorgensen, 492 P. 2d 312 (Or. App. 1971)
Pennsylvania - Commonwealth v. Taylor, 439 A. 2d 805 (Pa Super 1982)
South Carolina - State v. Pierce, 207 S.E. 2d 414 (1984)
Tennessee - State v. Glebock, 616 S.W. 2d 897 (Tenn. Cr. App. 1981)
Texas - Walters v. State, 680 S.W. 2d60 (Tex Cr. App. 1981)
Texas - Zani v. State, 679 S.W. 2d60 (Tex Cr. App. 1984)
Texas - Vester v. State, 713 S.W. 2d 930 (Tes App 1986)
Virginia - Hopkins v. Commonwealth, 337 S.E. 2d 264 (Va 1985)
Washington - State v. Martin, 684 P. 2d 651 (1984)
Washington - State v. Coe, 684 P. 2d 668 (1984)
Wisconsin - State v. Armstrong, 329 N.W. 2d 386 (1982)
Wyoming - Chapman v. State, 638 P. 2d 1280 (1982)

**Canadian courts**

Regina v. Pitt, 3 c.c.c. 342 11 C.L.Q. 120, 68 D.L.R. 2d 513

# chapter eleven

# The forensic session

On the day of the forensic hypnosis session (see Figure 11.1), the hypnotist should meet with the investigator before meeting the subject. During this meeting, the equipment will be set up and the hypnotist can explain how the session will be conducted so the investigator will be familiar with what will be expected of him if he is to assist in operating some of the equipment.

The hypnotist needs to make sure that the investigator understands that hypnosis does not solve crimes by itself. Anything obtained from the session must be corroborated by other evidence or testimony. Information gained from hypnosis does not carry any more weight in the justice system than information obtained by other means. Because of this, tangible evidence should be presented in support of the statements made during hypnosis.

One case which I assisted involved a subject exposing himself to high school students. The suspect waited until the high school let out for the day, at which time he would sit and watch for a group of high school girls to begin walking away from the school and head down some of the side streets near the school grounds. He then pulled up alongside the girls and begin to drive very slowly so they would notice him. When they did, he directed them to notice that he was not wearing any pants and that his genitals were exposed.

The detective on the case had attempted many different avenues to try to identify the suspect. None of the witnesses could remember the license number or give a very good description, because when the incidents occurred most of them ran away from the vehicle and the suspect quickly drove away. The detective talked to me about using hypnosis on several of his witnesses to see if this may help lead to some more details in the case.

During the sessions with several of the victims, none of them was able to provide a license number because no one looked at the back of the car. Most of them described the suspect and the interior of the car, which remained fairly consistent with each witness. The interesting observation was that each of the witnesses described the vehicle as being a different color — some said it was blue while others said green. This led to the possibility that the suspect was using two vehicles for his crime.

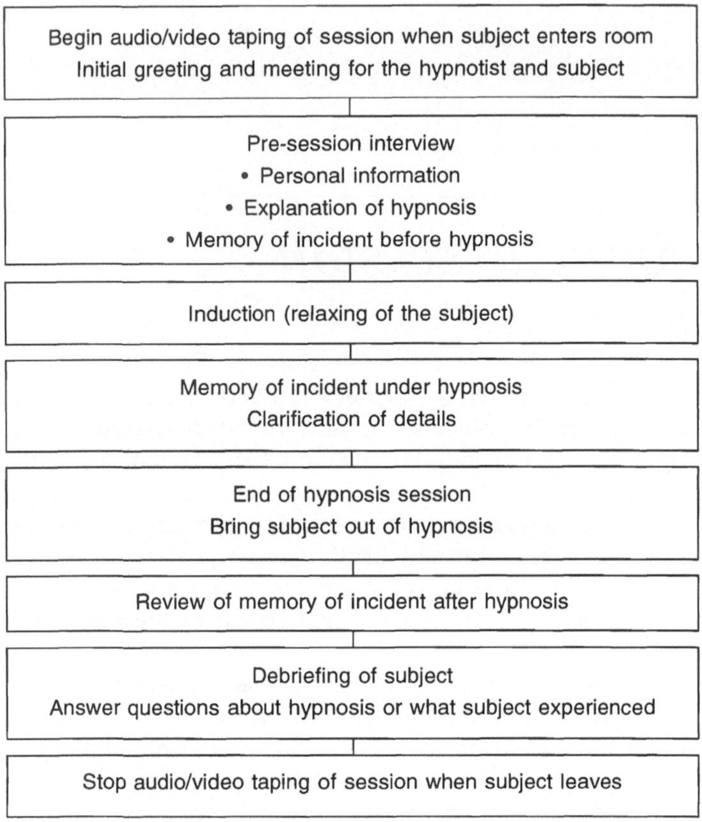


**Figure 11.1** Forensic hypnosis session.

Still, the session revealed no information at the time that would lead to a likely suspect in the case, and the detective went back to his traditional methods. His tenacity paid off, though, as a short time later he apprehended a suspect and found his vehicle. Depending on the way light hit the vehicle, it could look either blue or green. This allowed the detective to realize that there was only one car involved and he had the correct suspect.

Hypnosis did not solve this case, but because of the corroborating evidence the testimony of the witnesses had more credibility. That the vehicle had an odd paint color that changed depending on light conditions showed that the all witnesses were seeing the same thing.

In general, the number of individuals who attend a hypnosis session should be limited; however, the number of people attending can vary depending on the type of case and the subject. The most common number of individuals is three — the hypnotist, subject, and investigator, who also usually works the equipment. There can also be a sketch artist or composite operator on hand if the witness is going to be asked to describe a suspect.

Normally, there would be no other individuals permitted inside the forensic session so the subject will be able to relax and allow himself to go into hypnosis. If there are other individuals in the room who are not essential to the outcome of the session, then the room can take on a carnival-type atmosphere in which the subject will feel that he is on display, which could keep him from going into hypnosis.

I learned this the hard way. I worked on a case with the Bureau of Criminal Investigation in Ohio. In the room was the sketch artist, a victim's advocate, the subject, her spouse, and two detectives. The session resulted in minimal success. The subject was able to go under but only after a great deal of time had passed, and then she only remained in hypnosis for a brief time. There were too many people in the room and too many distractions for the session to be effective. In the case of the forensic session, less is better when it comes to people permitted to observe.

There are exceptions, of course, and if it eases the mind of the subject by having someone he knows and trusts present during the session, then it is all right, although not generally recommended. When permitting others to watch the session, you need to make sure that their presence is, in fact, what the subject desires. At one session I was conducting, a young woman brought her fiancé with her. When I met both of them I explained that the fiancé would have to wait outside until the session was finished. He became a little upset, saying that it was the subject's wish that he be present to watch over her. I was able to work out a compromise by having him wait outside the room but in front of a window to the room that allowed him to observe the proceedings. After he left the room and I began talking to the subject, I learned that she was not the one insisting he be in the room and that he was afraid that we (the investigator and myself) were going to "do something" to her. This is why it is best if the number of those attending be limited to those who must be there.

On occasion a child over the age of 5 will need to undergo hypnosis. If the child will not feel comfortable without a parent present, then make it a point to have the parent there. You need to have the parents' permission to hypnotize their child, anyway, so go ahead and ask them to attend. This often eases both their concerns and those of the child. An alternative to this would be to have the session in a location that has a two-way mirror allowing the guardian to observe the entire session. If this is done, then the child should be shown the room and assured that his parent is close at hand.

Just as you do not need extra family members and friends present during the session, you only need one investigator assigned to the case. More than one investigator will only add to the body count in the room and the uneasiness of the subject. More investigators wanting to observe the session is usually a case of them trying to satisfy their curiosity about hypnosis. It is better to let them watch the video tape than to satisfy these desires during the session.

Once the room has been set up with the recording equipment and it has been decided who will be permitted in the room, only then should the investigator bring the witness into the room. As soon as the subject enters the room, the recording equipment should be turned on so that when the introductions are made they can be recorded.

After that first "hello", the hypnotist goes to work and sets the stage for the session. It is this initial meeting that can move a session along rapidly or slow it down to where there is little chance of success. The forensic hypnotist must develop rapport with his subject just as for a clinical setting or even a stage hypnotist. Getting off to a bad start can delay progress, because the subject may not feel at ease with the hypnotist. A friendly, professional image will usually help the hypnotist survive this "first-impressions" part of the session.

Because the hypnotist does not know much about the case, some will want to make sure that the person they are working with is a victim or witness and not a suspect. The time to explore this possibility is during the rapport-building stage, before the session actually begins. Larry J. Hurley, a forensic hypnotist in Bellefontaine, Ohio, uses the following technique to assist him in forensic cases just to ensure he is not working with a suspect.

One of the first things Hurley does is to ask the subject who knows that he is there for the hypnosis session. Usually an honest person will discuss the hypnosis with friends. They may be a little apprehensive and will seek out the advice of others to see what they know about the subject. In contrast, a person who perhaps has some guilt associated with the situation under investigation may tend to keep to himself and not tell anyone about what he is about to do. This is not positive proof that a person is involved in the situation, but it is something to keep in mind.

Next Hurley asks the subject for his personal definition of the crime. People who are victims or witnesses will tend to describe an incident in more colorful terms, such as "robbed" instead of "theft", a term which might be used by a suspect. This is a normal response, as victims and witnesses tend to view the incident as a major event. A person involved in the crime will usually tend to down play the crime by using words such as "took" instead of "stole". Again, just because a person talks this way is not positive proof that he was involved in the crime. It just gives the hypnotist a chance to better evaluate the possibilities.

This line of questioning would be followed by an inquiry as to what sort of person might commit this type of crime. It must be fairly obvious by now as to what type of reaction you are looking for. A suspect in the crime may try to paint a picture of a sympathetic character as the perpetrator of the crime. A victim, of course, will have a much different version, and a witness will probably have an "I don't know" response or one that is similar to that of a victim.

Hurley then asks the subject how he thinks the suspect feels about the crime. Again, he would be looking for a sympathetic response on the part of a suspect or person involved in the crime. A boyfriend or girlfriend of a suspect who has been drawn into the crime investigation is likely to paint a

**Figure 11.2** During the interview phase, rapport is established between the hypnotist and the subject.

sympathetic image of the criminal. If the witness is not involved in the crime in any way, then this question will not affect the session, other than this question is asked during the rapport-building part of the session and any conversation helps to build that rapport.

The last inquiry Hurley makes regards what the subject feels should happen to the suspect. As you can imagine, by this point the victim will want justice by having the criminal prosecuted, as will a witness; however, a person involved with the crime may say, for example, that the criminal should receive counseling or an opportunity to return the stolen property and have the crime be forgotten.

If the hypnotist decides to explore whether or not the subject is a suspect and uses a technique like the one above or another, care should be taken so that a subject does not take offense to the questioning. This first part of the session, the interview, is extremely important for developing the rapport necessary for the session to continue (see Figure 11.2). This rapport building can involve any technique the hypnotist commonly uses to put people they meet at ease. Small talk and finding some common interest that helps to "break the ice" are good ways to begin. They also allow the subject to begin to get used to the hypnotist's voice.

The hypnotist should have a pre-printed interview form to follow which will help to ease some of the awkward tension found at the beginning of a session. This also allows the hypnotist to ask some common interest questions and allows the subject to begin to feel more at ease with the situation. The majority of individuals who come to a forensic session are going to be a little nervous and anxious about the whole situation. This is a common occurrence and it is based primarily on the many misconceptions about hypnosis.

A sample of an interview form (in the Appendix) has been provided to give a general idea of what kind of information the hypnotist needs to know before a session. Anything a hypnotist would like to add to such a form is fine. The routine questions included in the form allow subjects to become familiar with the sound of your voice and open up the session for conversation that will help relax the subjects and give you more information about them.

The form should include a place for the subject's name and address and other common information, such as some likes and dislikes. You should also learn whether or not the subject has been hypnotized before. All this information is important for designing your induction technique and for the explanation phase of the rapport building. You need to know a little about the subject's medical history, too. Finding out whether the subject suffers from such ailments as heart conditions, asthma, epilepsy, allergies, or others is important. These conditions normally will not be affected by hypnosis, but it is something you need to be conscious of during the session. One hypnotist failed to ask these medical questions and later told the subject to imagine himself in a hot air balloon that was coming down into a field of beautiful flowers. The subject started to sneeze and cough. When he came out of hypnosis, the subject told the hypnotist that he was allergic to certain types of field flowers. No harm was done, but a valuable lesson was learned.

You should also include questions about the subject's emotional condition. If the subject to be hypnotized is under the care of a psychologist or psychiatrist, then you should consult this doctor before doing the session. Unless you are one of these professionals, you will not be qualified to deal with the subject's problems that might emerge during the session. Remember, the responsibility for the session is yours, and the subject's welfare needs to be always at the forefront of your thoughts.

Another advantage to having a pre-interview form is that you will not forget to ask certain questions as you begin each session. It will also give you something to refer to during the session. Topics such as favorite colors and what the subject likes to do for relaxation can be brought up to help him relax during the induction segment.

Once the form has been completed and the subject has had a chance to get a little more comfortable with the situation, the hypnotist can now begin to explore the crime. Here is where the hypnotist hears for the first time all the details the subject remembers from the incident. Before any type of hypnosis is offered to the subject, he is asked to retell from his perspective as many details as he can about what took place. The hypnotist can ask any questions he wishes to during this period because the person is not hypnotized and the situation is the same as if an investigator were asking questions. The reason for doing this is to demonstrate what knowledge the subject was aware of before hypnosis. The court can also observe this session due to its being recorded and can consider testimony given prior to the aid of hypnosis.

In an attempted murder case I assisted, the subject, in this case the victim, had been counting money in the lower level of a bar when he was struck from behind with a blunt object, which brought him to the brink of death. When he was asked what he remembered about the incident before hypnosis, all he could say was that when he was counting money he felt a sharp pain in the back of his head, and then darkness closed in around him.

When he was in hypnosis, though, he told quite a different story. He remembered sitting at a table counting the money and then recalled a co-worker of his picking up a large pipe wrench and walking towards him. He could see this even though his back was turned because he noticed the co-worker's reflection in the mirror. He did not see the co-worker strike him, but he said that as he fell to the ground he noticed red splotches on his co-worker's white shirt.

This example shows clearly the difference between what a subject can remember before hypnosis and what he remembers during hypnosis. This is why it is important to document both memories so the court can see where the information was developed and how it was obtained. An interesting side note to this particular case is that when the subject was brought out of hypnosis he could not recall the details of the assault just as he had not been able to before hypnosis. He remembered talking about the attack but could not bring the images back into his mind after the hypnosis.

After the crime has been described in detail and before the hypnosis session can begin, the hypnotist needs to take the time to explain hypnosis to the subject. This is where information you learned in the earlier part of this book will come in handy. Give the subject a complete but brief explanation of how hypnosis works and explain that we all do it at least twice a day. Be as complete as the subject needs you to be. Encourage the subject to ask as many questions of you as he wants. Keep in mind that you want the subject to have the three items necessary for hypnosis: freedom from fear, willingness, and confidence. If the subject is too nervous about the idea of being hypnotized, he will not slip into it easily, if at all. This is the time to dispel any myths and present hypnosis in its true light.

You must see by now that much of the first part of the book has prepared you for this step in the process. Items that might not have seemed important, such as religious concerns, are now seen in a different light. There will be cases where witnesses will talk with their minister or religious leader and have many questions regarding their beliefs and hypnosis. Armed with the scientific approach and with the facts, you can put their minds at ease and show them that this natural tool will not alter their beliefs. They will be the same after hypnosis as they were before. You can also see how being able to respond immediately to the most common questions will help the subject gain confidence in you, which is invaluable in building the rapport necessary for hypnosis to occur.

During this part of the session you may want to explain all the stages of a hypnosis session and the techniques you are going to use. This will help the subject who may still be a little nervous. By being informed of each step, the subject will know where you will be taking him during the actual session. Knowledge always helps a person cope with a situation better, and the information you provide will show the subject that there will be no surprises coming out of the session.

Once the subject understands hypnosis and has no further questions, the actual session can begin. The hypnotist might want to make note of the time now, just as he should have when the session began. This keeps an accurate log of the total length of the session and at what point each part began and ended.

The next phase is the induction. Here is where easing the subject into hypnosis begins. Now that the subject has had the chance to hear about hypnosis and to get to know the hypnotist a little, the session can begin. Again, it is suggested that the time of the induction be recorded. If you do not remember what an induction is, refer back to the sample hypnosis session before reading on. The induction technique used in the sample is known as a general relaxation technique, which works fairly well on most individuals. The induction technique you choose can be one of many, whatever will work well with your subject. Here you can use the subject's likes and dislikes to help you provide a more comfortable setting.

When the induction is completed, make another notation on your pad as to the time you completed this portion. Now you are ready to deepen the hypnosis. Again, there are many varieties of deepening techniques and you should tailor yours to fit the subject. Earlier, an escalator technique was described which, again, normally works well for most. There is no need to take the subject very deep for a forensic session. Most people can refresh their memory very well with only a light trance.

An important point to make here is to never touch the subject during the hypnosis session without his permission. Some induction and deepening techniques that work very well involve touching a person's hand or shoulder. If you plan on using such a technique, you should always seek permission first and tell the subject that you will be touching him. In this manner, you maintain the subject's feeling of security and allow him to know your actions have a legitimate purpose.

In the next step — the reason for having the session — you will lead the subject back to the crime and ask him to tell you what he sees. A variety of ways are available to help the subject journey mentally back through time. One is to have the subject imagine a calendar with the dates going backwards, or have the subject walk down a tunnel toward the scene of the crime. Again, you are only limited by your imagination and that of the subject.

A word of warning: It is highly recommended that the victim of a violent crime not be asked to actually relive the crime. Depending on the crime, doing so can be very traumatic for the victim, because he will remember all of the emotions felt at the time, as well. A suggestion for victims of violent crimes is to have them imagine they are watching these events on a television or movie screen. With a technique like this they can remove themselves somewhat from the emotional trauma they have experienced, and you stand a better chance of having the subject remaining calm and retrieving the details that will assist in the investigation.

Once the subject has reached the crime scene, you have reached your objective. Here is where new information can be gained. Have the subject tell you the events of the crime again, just as you did earlier when he was not in hypnosis; however, do not ask leading questions. You may only ask what the subject sees, hears, smells, etc. The subject must be the one describing what is going on and providing the details.

It is at this point in the hypnosis session that a single wrong word could be shown in court to be a suggestion from you. This is why you must only use phrases such as, "What do you see now?" or "What is happening now?" With these kinds of phrases, the subject fills in the details and you do not offer any words that later can be construed as being suggestive. Remember that a defense attorney will attempt to discredit the hypnosis session, and the words you use during the session will be put under the closest scrutiny.

If the investigator in the room wishes to ask a question during the session, have him write it on a piece of paper so he does not speak. The hypnotist can read the question to himself and then see if he can get the subject to go where the investigator wants without leading the subject.

Suppose an investigator is interested in knowing whether the subject saw the license plate on the suspect vehicle. During the hypnosis session, the witness has described the vehicle, front, back, and sides, but has not touched on the license plate. The hypnotist could ask the subject something such as, "Take a moment and look at the back of the car. Describe to me everything you see in as much detail as possible so that I can see everything that you see." The witness in this example would then begin to describe the rear of the car. It is hoped that the license plate will be among the details, but if it is not, the hypnotist cannot come right out and ask about the license plate, because the witness might not have noticed the plate.

When you have gained all the information the subject has to offer, it is time to end the hypnosis part of the session. Count the subject out of the hypnosis with a simple count from 1 to 5, or any other similar technique. The counting-out phase does not have to be very long or intense, because the subject was never really asleep, is already relaxed, and has only to return mentally to where they are physically.

The last step is to have the subject go through the crime again now with his memory refreshed. Just as in the first phase you can now ask more pointed questions. These questions do not have to be limited, as they were during the hypnosis session, because the subject is no longer under hypnosis. Also, if the case investigator desires to ask some questions, this would be a good opportunity for him to do so. As we have noted already, the investigator should not ask questions during the hypnosis portion, because they may not use proper terminology and could place the entire session's admissibility in court in jeopardy.

Note on your pad the time the hypnosis session ended and the conclusion of the entire session when the subject walks out the door. Before the subject leaves, ask him if he has any questions about the session. The subject may want to comment on the sensation of hypnosis, and it will help if you address his questions, comments, or concerns rather than letting the subject wonder about them or seek answers from someone who is not informed on the subject. When the session is completed, you need to do as all investigators do — write a report and see that the tapes are secured in a property room and marked for evidence.

And that is how a forensic session is performed. You can see the differences between this type of session and the sample clinical session offered earlier. There are many more rules and guidelines to be followed during a forensic session, because the hypnotist must always keep in mind that the session must be admissible in court and the subject must not have his memory tampered with.

# *chapter twelve*

# *Inside the forensic session*

An understanding of hypnosis and the way it works combined with knowing how to perform a hypnosis session are only two components of the equation for a forensic hypnosis session. The third part is what occurs during the session itself, when the hypnotist attempts to extract information from the witness or victim. There are many variables and possibilities, and the hypnotist must be prepared to deal with them or the session will be unproductive. You may still have some questions at this point as to how to perform this part of the session in such a way as to ensure that the information is admissible in court. This is the crux of forensic hypnosis, because if the information is not admissible then it cannot help law enforcement or the victim.

After the hypnotist has performed the induction technique and has deepened the hypnosis using another technique (for this discussion, suppose that the escalator technique is being used), the subject is now at the bottom of the escalator and is stepping off. I tell him that he is stepping into a well-lit entryway, such as a hotel lobby (I always make sure to suggest that the way is well lit). Some people may not mentally turn lights on as needed, so they may feel as though they are walking down a dark hall, a feeling that could cause them to resist your suggestions. We want to make the experience as pleasant as possible for subjects, so you should be sure to turn on some lights for them. I might also mention that the floor is carpeted with extra padding so their steps are comfortable and the setting pleasing.

By this point, you should have decided how you are going to take the subject back in time, whether you are going to have him relive an incident or maintain some detachment by "watching" the incident play out on a "television screen", and where exactly the subject is going to go. For our discussion here, I am going to have the person relive an event, perhaps as a witness who was not really involved. During the pre-interview, I find that the subject likes to walk on the beach. So, once the subject has gotten down the escalator and arrived in the lobby, the session might go something like this:

> "As you enter the well-lit lobby, you see before you a set of double doors. You walk across the thick, plush carpet with extra padding and feel how cushioned your steps are. You reach the doors and easily push one open. Immediately you are basked in sunlight. The sun warms you and you feel more and more comfortable. As you look out before you, you can see the beach. The soft sand is inviting and you take your shoes off. You step out of the doorway and feel the warmth of the sand. It's warm and comfortable. As you walk along you can feel the sand between your toes. The sound of the waves fills your ears and you feel very comfortable and relaxed. You walk along the shore and the waves come up and touch your toes. The water is cool but comfortable against the warm sand. Above you can see a sea gull flying out for its morning search for food. You turn around and notice your footprints in the sand. Turning back you continue to walk along the water's edge. As you walk along you find yourself slipping back in time. Each step brings memories from the day before. These memories are vivid recollections as if they were happening now at the moment of the step. You continue to go back in time [at this point I would give dates, such as, 'It is now June 22, 21, 20, 15, 10, 5, 1, May 25']."

It should be noted here that it really does not matter how long ago the incident occurred. The best responses would probably come from a more recent date, but hypnosis has been successful in bringing forth details from older cases, as well.

> "Now we are at [insert the date here] and you look to your right, away from the beach. There sits a small building with a single door. You are drawn to this door and you walk away from the beach. Upon reaching the door you see something printed on its face. It says [insert date here]. You pull open the door and find yourself back in time to [insert the date; you will also want to supply the time or be prepared for getting a playback of their entire day]. As you enter the doorway and step back into time to [insert date] you look at your watch and see that it's [insert time of event]. You will be able to speak to me and describe all that you see just as it is happening. What's happening now?"

This is one way in which I have taken witnesses back in time to relive an event, but it is only one of many techniques you can use. The important thing to remember is to use information the subject tells you during the pre-interview. Let his likes and dislikes help you formulate induction, deepening, and time-travel techniques custom-made for him. This will make the journey easier for the subject because he will encounter situations to his liking, and the process will be easier for you because the subject will willingly go to your suggested place.

You may be wondering about suggestions possibly being given during this example. While it is true that during the hypnosis portion you are not to give any type of suggestions that will lead the subject, it is perfectly all right to give suggestions when trying to get the subject to go back in time. In the example given above, the suggestions offered about the sand, waves, sea gulls, and the door are all provided to assist the imagination of the subject. These suggestions are permissible because they are not suggestive of the crime and in no way offer suggestions pertaining to the crime itself. The important point here is that the portion of the session when the subject is offering information should be free of any type of suggestions, but the same is not true for the induction, deepening, or time-travel techniques.

Once you start to ask the subject what happened during the crime you must be very careful of your word choice. The wrong phrasing, as mentioned earlier, can rule the entire session inadmissible. Consider a forensic hypnosis session that involved the crime of rape. The hypnotist placed the victim under hypnosis and was guiding her through her day, up to the point that the rapist came into the scene. The suspect was walking up some steps and the victim was in her bedroom. The hypnotist referred to the suspect by name and asked the witness if the suspect was the man coming up the steps. Doing so, of course, was ruled inadmissible because it could be argued that the hypnotist planted the suggestion that the suspect was the rapist. So you can see how important your word choice is.

Your words during the session can also help remind the subject whether you want him to relive the event (as in the case of a witness) or merely watch it (as in the case of a victim). For example, asking a witness to describe what is happening to him now indicates that he is present at the crime scene while the particular incident is taking place. Asking questions phrased in the present tense places the subject at the scene, and asking the subject to describe what is taking place in front of him reinforces the suggestion that he is back in time and at the event.

Such a procedure is different from what you would want to use when dealing with a victim. In this case, you want to reinforce the fact they are just watching the event. So you want to ask the victim what he sees playing on a screen in front of him. This type of phrasing helps the victim remember that he does not have to allow himself to be emotionally involved with the events. This, of course, is difficult, but such a technique is more gentle than asking the victim to relive the event. The victim can observe the crime yet keep himself somewhat removed from the situation.

The words that a victim uses can assist you in knowing if he is simply remembering the crime or actually playing it out again in his mind as if it were happening all over again. Any use of the past tense during the victim's responses indicates he is remembering, which is not necessarily a failure. Remember that your goal is to enhance the victim's memory. Even if he is "just" remembering the event, details still may surface that were not remembered before. For a victim of a violent crime, this may be the best tactic to follow anyway. The hypnotist is there simply to help the victim remember the crime in more detail.

A subject who uses present tense in their responses is actually reliving the event. You will receive information just as it happened. When you get present-tense responses, make sure you respond in the present tense and ask questions such as, "What's happening now?" This will help keep the victim in the present. Again, you are only trying to refresh the memory, but if the victim relives the event in this way, then you have a good chance of uncovering forgotten information.

I was involved in a particular breaking-and-entering case in which the suspects entered a bank through the roof. The bank was located on the end of a shopping center strip. Several doors down was a Laundromat with an attendant. I was asked to work with the attendant, who might have seen something suspicious on the day the bank was broken into because the break-in occurred during daylight hours on a weekend. After the induction, I mentally took him back to the date and time and used the present tense to place him inside the Laundromat. The detective working the case was amazed at the events that then took place. The witness became very animated as he described what he was doing. He had been working on some books when the phone rang and he began a conversation with his friend. The entire conversation was repeated during this session, including the attendant noting that the power had gone out and his subsequent discussion of this outage with his friend. It was at this time, it turned out, that the suspects had cut into the power lines to shut off the bank's alarm system.

The witness then closed up the Laundromat, as he was the only one in there at the time, and had decided to go across the street to a gas station to get something to eat. As he walked into the gas station's lot, he observed a pick-up truck at one of the pumps. The truck caught his eye because it resembled a construction type of truck and he had heard some construction going on in the area. He also got a look at the driver and was a little afraid of the look he got back from this man.

The witness then returned to the Laundromat and resumed his telephone conversation, again commenting on the loss of power. Then the phones went out. As he sat in his chair describing these things to me, he suddenly jumped and tried to duck down in the chair. It took me several moments to figure out what he was doing. He related that as he stood there in the Laundromat that same construction truck drove by the front of the store very slowly and the driver looked in at him. The truck disappeared from view, only to return a minute later with the driver again looking in at him.

I asked the witness to go back to the first time he saw the truck and to describe it to me. He went back in time and read off the name on the side of the truck, complete with phone number, and he then went into detail regarding the body of the truck and the driver. As it turned out, the suspects used a construction company name on the side of their truck. The amazing thing about this session was that the witness relived it even down to the smallest details of his telephone conversations with his friend. This does not happen with all witnesses, but when a person relives an event it can be as rich in details as if it is happening at the moment.

People often forget details several minutes after an event because of all the activity going on around them. Many people also say they do not remember much because everything happened too fast. Under hypnosis, a subject can slow down an event so he can look around him and take in the details. To give the subject the ability to do this, all the hypnotist has to do is simply to tell the subject that he can, in fact, slow events down and take a closer look at them. Such a suggestion does not have any impact on the subject's statements about the event because the suggestions are all focused on the subject's being able to describe better what it is he is remembering. A method I have used in the past is to tell the subject that he is watching the events unfold before him but he is watching it on a film, a very special kind of film that will allow him to slow the action down or speed it up to suit his needs. I then ask him to review the "filmed" incident one frame at a time and to describe what he sees. The advantage of this is that it helps the subject realize he saw much more than he realized and can probably supply many more details about an incident than he expected.

Once you ask the subject what is taking place before him, be patient. Under hypnosis, responses tend to be slow in coming. If you start to ask too many questions or prod the subject repeatedly for information, you could become an annoyance and disturb the rapport you have built with him. Allow him to take time to answer. Usually the first response will be the slowest, while he is learning that he can speak and respond under hypnosis. Think back to a time when you were taking a nap and someone interrupted you. Your response was probably slow because you were relaxed. The same can be said for a subject in hypnosis. Patience is the key. Subjects should not be made to feel rushed, as they could become so tense that they come out of hypnosis.

When a subject starts to offer information, you can keep him going by asking what else he can tell you or what else he sees, hears, or smells. These types of phrases encourage the subject to give you information, as opposed to you asking direct questions such as inquiring about the license plate number on a car. By inquiring about a license plate before the subject tells you that he saw one, you are suggesting events that perhaps did not happen and could be jeopardizing the admissibility of the session in court. You must let the subject offer you the information.

Feel free to stop a witness any time you wish to know more. For example, let's say the witness to a murder says he is standing outside a store when he notices a man walk into the store. You can stop the witness at this point by saying, "I'd like you to stop right there and help me see what you see. Describe this man, telling me as much about him as you can so that I see everything you do." Then allow the subject to give you the description. Again, this would be perfectly admissible in court because all the information was provided by the subject. You did not offer any kind of suggestion here but merely tried to get the subject to pin down details.

Let's say the witness has finished his version of what happened and you want to go back over some earlier information. No problem — simply say something such as, "I'd like you to go back to [insert location, place, event, etc.] and look it over again. I'd like you to take your time and tell me everything you see, hear, or smell." Allow the subject time to review the scene again. If the subject has forgotten to tell you something the first time around, this additional opportunity may jog his memory. Of course, there is always the possibility that the subject did not see anything more.

One advantage to having the case investigator in the room with you is that they know everything that has been developed on the case so far. All that you, as the hypnotist, know are the date, time, and location of the incident and what the subject has told you. When an investigator decides he would like to know more about a certain detail and hands you his note with his request, you must be patient when trying to obtain the information. All you can do is have the subject return to the area in question and then try to narrow down what he is looking at.

Let's return to the previous example regarding the witness standing outside a store. Suppose the detective has handed you a note that read, "Mask or no mask?" The witness to this point has not mentioned any type of headgear on the subject. You could say something such as, "I'd like you to go back to when you had the best possible look at this person and just hold that image in your mind. Now that you have his image I want you again to start at the top and work your way down, giving me everything you see so I can see what you see." Then let the witness describe the scene again. A bad way of approaching this (and one that will be challenged by a defense attorney) would be to say, "I want you to go back to when you had the best view of the subject and just hold that in your mind. Now that you have that image, I want you to tell me what is on his head or covering his face." See the difference? In the first example, you let the subject tell you what was there. In the second example, you are planting the idea that there must be something there. Big mistake for a forensic hypnotist. Again, the hypnotist must allow the subject to provide the information.

You can have the subject go back over the information as much as you desire, but the effectiveness of this will be limited. Usually, if you are going to gain any fresh information it will appear in the first couple of "visits" to the scene. However, after the session is completed, remind the subject that he may remember more over the next day or so now that his memory has been refreshed. If he does remember something else, he should contact the investigator about it, no matter how trivial the detail may seem. It is not uncommon for witnesses to come up with details later, after their subconscious minds have started to review the crime and the scene.

If you are using such imagery as a television screen, you have yet another technique at your disposal to help draw out new details. You can tell your subject that he is looking at a special type of television set. He can zoom in, if he needs to, or zoom back out. Whatever he needs the television set to do, it can do it. Now, suppose you want the subject to describe a license plate. Simply tell the subject to zoom in on the plate and tell you what he sees. Again, you must be careful not to plant ideas in the subject's head, but do allow him to tell you what he sees when he zooms in.

You can also ask the subject to let the screen go blank. When it comes back on again, the license plate will be there in front of him. Now let him tell you what he sees. Again, the witness must tell you first that he has, indeed, seen a license plate; otherwise, you would be planting the suggestion in their head.

You are limited only by your imagination and the fact that you cannot make suggestions to the subject. When you are trying to elicit information during the session you can transfer the rapport to someone else simply by saying, "Now, [insert subject's name], I'm going to let you talk to [insert name]. They have some things they'd like you to explain to them about this incident, too. Is that okay?" Always get the consent of the subject before doing anything like this. Also, keep in mind that when you transfer rapport, you run the risk of someone else asking a suggestive question. If you are going to transfer rapport during a forensic session, make sure you have sat down with this person and gone over the type of questions he can ask. You do not want the entire session being ruled inadmissible because an untrained person asked the wrong kind of question. What is meant by "rapport" here is the voice the subject will concentrate on when spoken to. Going under hypnosis, the subject focused on the voice of the hypnotist, but after the session is on going and the rapport has been transferred, the subject will focus on the second voice.

An example of when a hypnotist might turn over the session to someone else would be when they are working with an artist. The subject will be asked to open his eyes and examine what the artist has drawn from the description the subject has provided so far, but sometimes the artist has questions he would like answered so he can enhance the drawing. When I work with an artist, I get together with the artist prior to the session and go over the information he will want to learn during the session, and then I phrase the questions myself during the session while the artist remains quiet. This, however, is a time when the hypnotist may choose to transfer the rapport.

Another time could be when there are two hypnotists working together on a session, and they switch off during various parts of the session.

As a general rule, I do not let anyone else ask questions during the session. In this manner, I am able to keep a careful watch over what is said and in this way keep some quality control over the suggestions offered. Remember the responsibility for the session lies with the hypnotist.

Sometimes the subject can see something but is not be able to describe it fully for the hypnotist. For example, in a theft case I worked on, the suspects drove into a lumber yard in a pick-up truck with the tailgate down. While they loaded some lumber onto the truck, the witness, who was an employee of the lumber company, went out to them with some twine to help them tie down the load. They then drove away. Problem was, they did not pay for any of the lumber.

Under hypnosis the employee remembered that the truck was a powdery blue and that there was no front license plate. He also remembered that all of the suspects had been drinking a popular brand of beer and still had some with them in the truck. There were four suspects altogether, with one behind the driver's seat and three outside of the truck when the witness approached. While he described the rear of the truck, I wanted him to focus on the license plate, but I had to wait until he brought the subject up himself. At last he mentioned that the license plate was obstructed by the lumber hanging over the bed of the truck. I asked him to describe what he was able to see of it, but he stated that he could not make it out.

Not wanting to give up on this, I had the employee open his eyes and draw on a piece of paper exactly what he had seen regarding the license plate. He drew a line that represented the tailgate of the truck and then proceeded to fill in the bottom half of several of the digits in the plate. I then asked him to close the tailgate, look at the license plate, and write down the number. He hesitated a moment, but then he complied with my request by filling in the numbers and a letter as best he could based on what he had seen. Even he had to admit after the session that he apparently had seen quite a bit more than he thought he did (see Figure 12.1).

I used a similar technique when working with a witness to a homicide for a neighboring jurisdiction. The witness was in an apartment, looking out from a second-floor window, and as she watched her husband was murdered by two suspects. As she described the incident it was found that both men wore ski masks and that one had a handgun of some kind. Because she was not able to describe verbally the style and type of masks, I asked her to sketch these objects, which she did. Although these sketches would not lead directly to the suspects' arrest, they could offer valuable information relating to the development of suspects.

There is no better teacher than practice. It is always a good idea to practice any type of skill. Being able to phrase things in a way that is not suggestive is not as easy as it seems. Work with a friend to see how you are doing. A simple exercise is to have a friend tell you something he did that

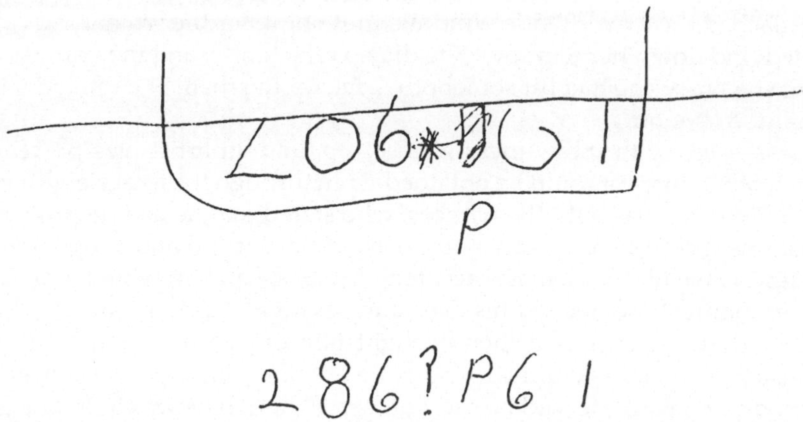

**Figure 12.1** Witness' drawing of license plate numbers after having memory refreshed by hypnosis.

day. Then try to go back and gather more details about it without suggesting any particular thing.

There are times when things do not go exactly as you have planned or expected them to. The hypnotist must be prepared to deal with such occasions. For example, as discussed earlier, the subject might begin to have a reaction during hypnosis, and the hypnotist must end the session by taking the subject deeper and then bringing him out. There are other problems, too, that can startle the hypnotist.

Consider the subject who opens his eyes right in the middle of the session. Did he bring himself out of hypnosis? I do not know for sure. In some instances, the subject has opened his eyes and is fully alert and awake, just as he was before the session began. Other times, though, I have merely held up my hand and asked the subject to close his eyes, only to discover that he is still deep in hypnosis. If the subject suddenly opens his eyes, it is always best to have him close his eyes and then either bring him up and out of hypnosis or continue on. If you have decided to end the session, then it can be shown that you verbally gave the subject the instruction to come out of hypnosis. On the other hand, if you have decided to keep the subject in hypnosis, continuing on could reveal what perhaps startled him into opening his eyes.

In a particular vehicular homicide case I had the opportunity to assist, two women were crossing the street early in the morning, walking from one bar to another. As they neared the middle of the street, a car pulled out of one of the bar parking lots and struck one of the women, driving over her and continuing on down the road. A witness was driving in that same direction and saw the whole accident. After stopping to check on the victim, he drove down the street and caught up to the car at a red light. He exited his car and approached the driver's side window, motioning for the woman driving the car to wind down her window. She did so reluctantly, and the witness asked her if she knew she had hit somebody back up the road. She replied she had not and drove off.

A session with the witness was set up, and an artist was present so a sketch of the suspect could be obtained. I ran through the interview sheet and discussed hypnosis with the witness, who stated that he had no problems or questions. The session began, and I used the induction and deepening techniques to take him back to the accident. I then asked him what he saw. After a brief moment, he opened his eyes and said this was not working. I asked him to close his eyes and then brought him out with a count of five. My curiosity made me ask him why he came out of hypnosis, especially since he seemed so relaxed. He said he did not feel as though he was in hypnosis and it certainly could not have been very deep. His expectations had not been met, even though I had explained to him that there would not be a trance. Because he did not experience the trance he expected, the witness brought himself out of hypnosis.

The story does not end there, though. I still had him work with the artist and they developed an excellent sketch of the suspect. When she was later arrested and the sketch was placed next to her photograph, many commented on how similar the images were, almost as if she had posed for the drawing.

The effectiveness of hypnosis with this subject is open to debate. Would he have been able to describe the suspect in so much detail before the hypnosis session? We do not know for sure, but he had not been able to provide very much detail prior to the session. Did the hypnosis refresh his memory and allow him to offer so much detail? We do not know that, either, but the important thing is the results came out of the hypnosis session, which was properly recorded so the court could see how the information was obtained.

Another example of an odd response to hypnosis was a case of two missing children that the FBI asked me to assist on. The children had been missing for several weeks, and there were no leads in the case. A witness said he remembered seeing a car parked in the driveway of the children's home a few days before their disappearance, and he remembered looking at the car but could not remember much about it.

During the interview phase, I found out that this witness was a hunter and he enjoyed spending time in the woods. Using this information, I described a path in the woods to him after I performed the induction and deepening techniques. As he walked along the path, I told him that he was going back in time, and I walked him back to the date and time the car was seen at the children's house. I told him that when he stepped out of the woods he would be at the children's house, and I then asked him what he saw. His response was that he saw nothing. I asked him what he was doing. His reply was just as disheartening as his earlier response. He said he was sitting there listening to me. Realizing that I may not have been able to help this witness into hypnosis, I talked him out with a count of five. When he was fully alert, I asked him if he could tell me what happened and whether he had seen the woods that I had described to him. His face brightened, and he said that he had seen the woods and there were deer there. I had not described any deer, but his imagination had filled them in. I then asked him what happened when he stepped out of the woods, and he said that he just went blank.

Was the witness in hypnosis? Yes, because he was able to describe the woods and he even added things normally found in a woods but not described by the hypnotist. Why the witness did not go back and retrieve information about the car is a mystery to me and can only be answered by the witness. No new information was gained from this session. Such results (or lack of) are part of the reality for the hypnotist. But the hypnotist can only do so much for the subject. He cannot make the subject remember events or details that are known only by the subject. Investigators may sometimes think the hypnotist has failed, but as long as the hypnotist has followed proper procedures, the results rest with the subject alone.

A possible alternative to a session ending with no results can be found in a technique developed in 1984 by Martin Reiser, Director of Behavioral Science Services for the Los Angeles Police Department, and researchers from the UCLA Department of Psychology. This procedure is called the cognitive interview, which tries to help the witness retrieve minute details *without* using the induction and relaxation techniques necessary for hypnosis. There is a nine-step process for this technique, which has been shown to be able to retrieve details just as hypnosis does. And, like a hypnosis session, a cognitive interview requires some time and patience to obtain all of these details.

In the beginning, the witness reconstructs the circumstances surrounding the incident. The interviewer does not want to start with the incident itself, but rather with something normal in the person's life. So the witness may talk about driving down the road to pick the kids up at school when she saw a truck strike a car coming out of a side street. This gives the interviewer an overview of the situation and allows the witness to begin to think of her day not so much in regard to the incident but to her normal routine.

The interviewer then explains to the witness that she needs to tell everything about the incident. She should not hold anything back, even if she feels it is unimportant. All details should be brought forth. Then the interviewer has the witness describe the incident again but this time he asks questions in the present tense regarding such things as the weather, time of day, and people who might be around so that the witness begins to think in detail and in the present tense, which keeps her mentally at that point and time.

The interviewer then asks the witness to recall the events in a different order. For example, the interviewer could have the witness start at the end and work backward or in the middle and go forward. This makes the witness think harder, and the interviewer can ask questions such as what happened just before the car came onto the street.

Then the interviewer asks the witness to change her perspective and to describe the incident from this new point of view. The witness could be asked to look at it from across the street or even from the perspective of one of those involved in the incident. This again makes the witness concentrate, and she is encouraged to offer as many details as she can, holding nothing back.

Only after the incident has been described in as much detail as the witness can offer does the interviewer begin to zero in on the participants' descriptions. The first area is physical appearance. The interviewer asks the witness to describe the people involved but not in the standard way of typical police interviews. Instead, the interviewer asks the witness if the people remind her of anyone and, if so, why. People are often described as being similar to someone famous because of their apparel, walk, hair style, or looks. The interviewer tries to get the witness to offer as much as she can about the physical appearance of everyone involved.

If a name was given during the incident, the witness would then be asked to begin thinking of names beginning with the first letter of the alphabet and then to continue working her way through the alphabet, stopping at any names that fit. In this way, the interviewer can determine how many syllables the name had and narrow down the letter with which the name started.

Speech characteristics are the next focus. The interviewer asks if the witness heard an accent or if the way a person spoke sounded similar to anyone she knows personally or who is famous. This, again, is an attempt to jog the witness' memory to see if more can be brought out.

The last phase of the cognitive interview is to discuss any conversations that took place during the incident. All individuals have particular speech patterns and phrase things in certain ways, and the witness is asked if she can recall any of recognizable speech patterns. Perhaps someone's tone of voice stood out, especially if the person was stressed during the incident. Again, the witness is asked if the speech patterns she heard resemble those of anyone she knows or who is famous.

The cognitive interview does not raise so many questions in court, because the subject is not in hypnosis but is fully alert and relaxed. If a hypnosis session was not able to bring about the desired results, then the cognitive interview offers another opportunity to uncover the desired details.

# chapter thirteen

# Professional ethics

Every professional organization has a code of ethics the members are expected to follow, and this is especially true for the various branches of the criminal justice system. Because of the difficult path hypnosis has had to follow down through the centuries, ethical hypnotists follow a code of ethics which sets them apart from others who are less interested in acting in a professional manner. The hypnotist who takes on the role of being a forensic hypnotist must hold himself accountable to this high standard for several reasons.

To even be considered by the law enforcement community to work with them on a criminal case, the hypnotist must have a solid reputation. Traditionally, the police have been very conservative in their approach to investigating criminal complaints and with good reason. Only tried and tested methods are utilized because the success of each case depends on the best methods available. To many detectives, the idea of using hypnosis is the same as asking a magician to pull a suspect out of a hat. The information gained from hypnosis can neither be touched nor seen and therefore is subject to debate. The idea of turning over their only witness to a person who makes people bark like dogs on a stage would be unthinkable to an investigator unless that hypnotist has had the opportunity to explain how he is different and to show their abilities in a professional manner.

Another reason the forensic hypnotist needs to follow this ethical path has to do with the attorneys assigned to the case, both for the prosecution and the defense. The prosecutor will want to know the scientific applications of hypnosis. He will also expect the hypnotist to be a person that the prosecutor can place upon the stand in court without worrying about his testimony being questioned because of his character. The defense attorney might attempt to portray hypnosis in a less than favorable light by taking advantage of popular misconceptions about it, and in doing so might hope to discredit the hypnotist. Thus, only a professional and ethical hypnotist can expect to make a contribution to law enforcement.

The witnesses or victims will also need to know something about the hypnotist. For them to have confidence in the hypnotist, the reputation of that hypnotist can be nothing other than professional. Because confidence in the hypnotist is one of the three items necessary for hypnosis to take place, it is also key to the high ethical standards of a forensic hypnotist.

For the sake of this text, suppose you have won the approval of an investigator, who has entrusted you with his witness or perhaps you are an investigator, qualified in hypnosis, who has been asked by another investigator to consult on a case ... either way, when it comes to the hypnosis session you must understand that you are responsible for that session. You are the trained and experienced person in the matters of hypnosis. You cannot compromise your principles or how the session is conducted, no matter what kind of pressure might be applied by others.

This is the first mile marker on the code of ethics for a hypnotist who works with law enforcement. They assume the entire responsibility for how a session is conducted and what occurs in that session, just as the investigator who took on the case has the responsibility for how the complaint will be investigated, and the prosecutor decides how the case will be presented. The hypnotist cannot pass this responsibility on to anyone. When the forensic hypnotist is on the witness stand, it will be up to him to answer the technical questions regarding how the session was conducted. Be forewarned, if you have compromised your ethics and done something unethical, you will be questioned about it on the witness stand and you can be sure that the defense will have another hypnotist on hand to question your methods. It is best to play by the rules and to let the case move in the direction indicated by the evidence. This applies to any specialist in the criminal justice field. The polygraph examiner is responsible for the polygraph test and the manner in which it was performed. The lab technician who processes evidence and determines the origin of such things as blood samples must also account for his methods of testing. The same holds true for the hypnotist.

Along with this responsibility comes the understanding that you must represent yourself accurately as to who and what you are and what you can and cannot do. Do not say you have experience in an area where you do not. Misrepresentation of you or your abilities will only harm the use of hypnosis by those who are qualified to do so. The reading of a few books and practicing on some friends do not make you a hypnotist, especially one ready for the rigors of a forensic session.

The forensic hypnotist must stick with the areas of hypnosis in which he is competent. In an earlier chapter, we discussed staying within your area of expertise — for example, a hypnotist who does not hold a Masters or is not a psychiatrist or psychologist would not use hypnosis for therapy and cannot call himself a hypnotherapist. The forensic hypnotist must be sure he never gets involved in matters outside of his expertise, because his credibility is at stake. By realizing his limitations, the hypnotist ensures that he is perceived as an ethical and competent individual. It may mean that he will not be able to help someone with a particular problem, even though he may want to. He should either refer this person to someone who *is* capable of dealing with the situation or advise them as to why you can offer no assistance. In the long run, others will respect you more for it.

You should be willing to work with other professionals as required by the situation. For example, if a person desires to have his psychologist with him during a session because he suffers from a neurosis of some kind, allow yourself to be flexible. This would particularly apply if you are not qualified to treat the type of affliction affecting the subject. If it will help the case you are working on and will provide a safe environment for the witness, then by all means allow the psychologist to be present and ask for guidance from him when necessary. You will need his permission to use hypnosis on his client, anyway, so it would be in your best interests (as well as those of the subject) to work with the other specialist. Before the session, however, establish ground rules with the other specialist to maintain the admissibility of statements made during the session. Establish a cue to let the other specialist know that he is to step in and assist should his expertise become necessary.

You need to keep your subject's welfare at the forefront of any hypnosis session. You should not get caught up in the "we've got to get the evidence" mentality. The subject needs you to monitor the session, which goes back to your being responsible for the session. If a person begins to display some kind of abreaction, then you need to respond to it immediately without any panic, even if you have not been able thus far to gain the knowledge being sought during the session. Remember, this person is trusting you to guide him safely back to the crime scene to remember what happened. If he gets into some kind of trouble before or during that, it is you who must act to end the session. Your responsibility is to ensure that the session is professionally performed and that the subject's well-being takes precedence.

An example of a subject's welfare becoming the top priority can be found in a robbery case I assisted with. A woman was an employee of a small Italian restaurant which also had a small lounge. One evening shortly before closing, a man entered the restaurant armed with a gun. Most of the staff had already left, and only this woman remained to lock up for the evening. The man took the night's receipts and physically injured the woman.

As I prepared to begin the session, the woman offered this very information. I had already been given the date, time, and location by the investigator and had completed the interview form. I began with the general relaxation technique offered in an earlier chapter. All seemed to be going well. Her breathing had slowed, even though she had been very nervous prior to discussing hypnosis with me. I wanted to take her a little deeper and tried to use the escalator technique to have her descend five floors. As I began this technique, though, her body seemed to tense up. I thought it odd but continued, this time offering words of support and telling her all was well. She shook her head once, and I decided she should be brought out of hypnosis.

I discussed the reactions I had observed with her and asked her what she was thinking or feeling during the escalator description. She then explained to me that the suspect made her go down into the basement of the restaurant and that is where he hit her. She was afraid she was going to die when he followed her down there, and the escalator had reminded her of what had happened. Information about the basement had not been offered to the detective prior to the session, so he and I were hearing it for the first time.

The peace of mind and safety of your subject must come first, even if it means stopping the session and not being able to help the investigator. The forensic hypnotist must also hold himself to a high moral code. The use of hypnosis must be kept at a professional level. The hypnotist must be conscious of the fact that his actions outside of the forensic setting can bring discredit to hypnosis and to his character. For these reasons, the hypnotist must not use hypnosis in a way that is unethical or conduct himself in a manner during a hypnosis session that could cast doubt upon his moral code of ethics.

One of the most frequent attacks on hypnotists is their being accused of unwanted sexual advances. Claims have been made by subjects (usually of the opposite sex of the hypnotist) that during their sessions the hypnotist made some sexual suggestions. Whether or not the allegations made in these cases are true or not, hypnotists must take precautions against such claims by not making any sexually suggestive comments during the hypnosis session and by protecting themselves in some way against such claims. One method, offered earlier, is to have a witness present who is the same sex as the person being hypnotized. If a person of the same sex as the subject is not available, then a second option is to have a witness who is the same sex as the hypnotist. This option is not as desirable as the first, but it is still an easy method to prevent claims of this sort. Protection is also offered by video and audio tapes of hypnosis sessions. Such tapes, along with the testimony of witnesses, should be more than sufficient to show that no unwanted sexual advances were made during hypnosis sessions in question. The forensic hypnotist, as is true for all ethical hypnotists, must be above reproach on this issue. It only takes one who crosses the line to cast doubt on all of the others. Just as all professionals are judged by the actions of one, so too are hypnotists. It just makes good sense not to be the one who brings shame to the profession.

Another mile marker on this ethical road is following legal standards and guidelines. When taking on a forensic case, whether the hypnotist is a law enforcement officer, psychologist, psychiatrist, or other person trained in hypnosis, they have taken on the role as a participant in the criminal justice system and must act according to its guidelines. A hypnotist not following these guidelines could lead to entire sessions being inadmissible in court and would result in a waste of time for the investigators and witnesses.

Just as for doctor-patient or a lawyer-client relationships, the hypnotist-client relationship must be assumed to be confidential. For the forensic hypnotist, this is even more so. The hypnotist cannot go about discussing a case he has worked on while the case is still under investigation. He also cannot tell the public what goes on during hypnosis sessions and who his subjects are without the approval of the subject and case investigator. This would be expected from any professional, and the hypnotist is no exception. The forensic setting is to be kept confidential between the police, hypnotist, and subject, and only when the case is presented in court or disposed of should the details of that session be shared.

Think about how important confidentiality is to a hypnotist. The investigator must have faith in your confidentiality to trust you with the case, and you must have a strong moral code for the subject to confide in you. You must stay within your area of expertise for the prosecutor to be willing to put you on the witness stand, and you must be willing to assume responsibility for the hypnosis session. The subject of ethics is not one you can just talk about and automatically acquire by doing so. It is the way in which you conduct yourself and the path you follow that determine whether you are ethical or not. Taking the easy way on a case or bending the rules set down by the court will erode your ethics until gray and black all seem the same.

If you are a law enforcement officer or work for a prosecutor's office and you perform hypnosis, you must follow the guidelines of your agency. If there is no general order or guideline established by your agency, it will be in your best interest as well as your agency's to have written rules to govern a hypnosis session. This will clarify what is expected from the hypnotist, investigator, and others involved with the case. It will also help supervisors maintain a checks-and-balances system for the individuals who work with hypnosis. Should a person step outside of the guidelines, then the agency will have a chance to address the problem before the individual has a chance to discredit an effective tool for law enforcement. The professional representation of hypnosis is the only way this tool will gain greater acceptance by law enforcement.

In this day and age, when everyone seems intent on gaining notoriety in the media (be it the evening news or movies and television), you should strive to maintain a professional image within the media. Do not expect to become a star just because you understand how this tool works. That would be the same as a person who operates a polygraph trying to cash in on the cases with which he was involved.

Let's return to the subject of the media. As I have mentioned, the media often portray hypnosis in a poor light. When a newsperson hears that the police are going to use hypnosis in a criminal case, his interest is piqued because this would seem to be a different and unusual police procedure. If you find yourself the subject of an interview about the use of hypnosis for a specific case, approach the opportunity as a professional. When discussing hypnosis, remember your training and explain the hypnosis procedures clearly. You are representing everyone who uses forensic hypnosis when you are asked to speak about it. What a person in authority says can have far-reaching implications for courtroom testimony for years to come.

The individuals who present the evening news and write for the local newspaper can be considered as double-edged swords, so the hypnotist must be careful. Because the news people are in the business of selling newspapers or promoting their news show, they may be tempted to sensationalize hypnosis in order to create a demand for their paper or to entice viewers to tune in to their show. They do this without regard to the impact their actions may have on the reputation of hypnosis and the hypnotist's career. In contrast, the media can also make the public aware of accurate and useful information about hypnosis and eliminate many of the myths about hypnosis that persist. But, the hypnotist should be careful in his dealings with the media and should ask to see an article before it is published or broadcast, although there have been times when a writer has submitted a story to his editor only to have the editor change it because he thought it might read better if some of the information in the original story was changed.

As an example of the media not fully appreciating the sensitivity of hypnosis and law enforcement, a television station reporter called to make a request of me. The station was doing a show on hypnosis and the use of it in criminal cases. They were looking for information about individuals who had been hypnotized and the kind of information that had been gained from the sessions. At first this station's request seemed like a good opportunity to help the public see and understand how hypnosis works.

The reporter then proceeded to tell me that they were already interviewing a person about the use of forensic hypnosis, and this hypnotist had been quite helpful, but there was a problem. Their forensic hypnotist could not offer any names of people to be interviewed about their forensic hypnosis sessions. The reporter wanted me to dig through my cases to give her the names and telephone numbers of some of the witnesses with whom I had performed forensic hypnosis so they could be called and interviewed. Apparently their "forensic hypnotist" had never performed a hypnosis session in a criminal case, yet the television station was about to put him on their evening news and present him as an expert. To top it off, they wanted to use my witnesses without interviewing me in the process.

I had to give them credit for their enthusiasm and optimism, of course, but I did not give them any witnesses' names or phone numbers, as doing so would have been unethical and would ruin my credibility with the law enforcement community. But this experience does serve as an example of how the media do not always care about presenting all the facts about a subject. The hypnotist, though, must remain on the lookout for his own agenda, his reputation, and the security of his witnesses.

To counter misinformation about hypnosis, you may want to write some articles on the subject. Local newspapers may be willing to accept articles submitted by a respected source, and this is a great way to educate many about the scientific approach to hypnosis. Keep in mind, though, that whatever you put into print can be subject to criticism from all sides. There will be hypnotists who are not as ethical who may try to counter your assertions.

The media may try to get you to phrase things in such a way that they can turn your words around to take on an entirely new meaning. You need to be careful, therefore, in regard to the words you use when you write an article. If you stay within the scientific approach and present hypnosis as it really is, you should have no trouble. Ethical hypnotists are the best publicity a tool such as hypnosis can have. The more discussion there is about hypnosis being an effective tool that follows established guidelines, the more readily law enforcement and the courts will regard it as an acceptable practice.

There are other professional considerations you will want to keep in mind. One of the first is to maintain your credibility. You need to be aware of your limitations in regard to the use of hypnosis and should perform hypnosis only to the fullest extent of your training. If you have not been trained in clinical hypnosis, then do not attempt to perform clinical hypnosis. If you have not been trained in forensic hypnosis, do not attempt it. Keep in mind that if you perform hypnosis on someone experiencing a problem possibly linked to a biological cause and you have not consulted the subject's physician, you are practicing medicine without a license. Resist the temptation to treat people for pain, headaches, etc. without consulting their doctor.

Also resist trying to combine a clinical session with a forensic session. For example, during a session for witness memory do not give the subject suggestions for overcoming a habit of some kind, such as smoking. This will confuse the issue in court and is not what you are there for. If the subject contacts you after the case and asks you to help him in an area for which you are qualified, then by all means help him. In the forensic setting your primary goal is to assist the witness in remembering clearly the events, people, and places that were involved in the crime. To do any more than that takes away from the quality of the work and opens the session up to more criticism and attack from a defense attorney and other skeptics.

Hypnosis is not going to help every case. If you are an investigator and are trained in hypnosis, do not think it offers an answer to all your problems. Hypnosis, after all, is simply a tool, and like all tools there are certain times and places when they are effective. Use the tool properly, and you will get the results you are looking for more often than not. If you use a tool such as hypnosis when it is not appropriate, though, you may find that the tool has not served you well, that you have steered others away from using the tool, and that confidence in the tool has been lost by the people for whom the tool was designed to help.

Think about if you, as a police officer, were to pull out your baton in every situation where force was needed. You would soon learn it does not work every time. There would be times when the baton was too much force, and times when the baton was not enough force to get the job done. There is a time and place to use the baton, and the same is true for hypnosis.

Be on guard against competitiveness. Growing up in a world in which sports can have a major impact on our character, it is easy for each of us to develop a competitive drive. We each want to succeed and do better than the next. As a forensic hypnotist, you cannot afford to feel as though you are in a competition with the investigating officer to solve the crime. You are there as an assistant, to glean vital details that will bring about an arrest and a cleared complaint. Keep your personal drives and feelings under control, and always remember that you are a professional being asked to perform a service and to help prevent an offender from getting away.

Along those lines, keep yourself in check. It is very easy for any of us to become impressed with ourselves. This idea of grandiosity does not serve the interests of hypnosis, especially forensic hypnosis. If you find yourself thinking that you are very important, remember that all you have is a little bit of training; it is the witness who controls the hypnosis session. If a subject wanted to, he could make you look very foolish simply by just sitting there during a session and not doing anything you have asked of him. You have no power; you are not in control of anyone. All you have are some skills that can help another person. Those who place themselves too high on a pedestal usually fall the hardest when they topple. Keep a firm check on yourself and your abilities, and always keep in mind why you are in the hypnosis session in the first place.

A warning that is issued to most individuals involved with counseling or the healing arts is not to become emotionally involved with the witness or client. This is very important, because should it happen you need to be able to recognize it immediately and take steps to prevent the involvement from developing further. The rapport developed during the hypnosis session between hypnotist and subject can be very strong. This strong rapport can be misconstrued by both the hypnotist and the subject. If you allow yourself to believe this rapport is something more than what it is, you will find your judgment on the issue becoming cloudy. It will affect your dealings with the subject and may taint your session, not to mention your career. Be professional and remain professional by always remembering the purpose of the session and the reason for your involvement with the case. Many doctors will tell you that a strong bond between physician and patient can sneak up on them and a situation quickly develops that is not healthy for the doctor (hypnotist) or the patient (subject). Just keep in mind that you are only there as a guide and nothing more.

One last item for you to consider as a professional in the hypnosis community: Keep yourself educated on the subject. What we know about hypnosis is nothing compared to what we do not know. Every year there are new discoveries on the subject. You should read current books on the subject as well as attend professional workshops and subscribe to professional journals that pertain to hypnosis. Most professionals, especially physicians and attorneys, constantly read to keep themselves up to date. If you believe that after you have received training in basic and advanced hypnosis you know all you will ever need to know, you are in for a rude awakening. As others discover new techniques and new ways in which the human mind can work, you will be left behind. An example of this can be found in the healing arts.

Hypnosis has been used on patients who suffer from cancer. The results so far seem promising, as hypnosis has helped patients deal with the pain, has helped the body recover from the effects of treatments, and in some cases even seems to have helped the body fight the disease. But, if you do not attend seminars or read the new information available, you will never know of advances like these. Who knows, 10 years from now the way we perform hypnosis may look like Mesmerism when compared to new methods. You do not want to stay in the Dark Ages, do you?

The main point raised by this chapter is that when you perform hypnosis, especially in a forensic situation, you represent all hypnotists. It takes the unprofessional actions of only one to ruin it for all. Hypnosis is a tool that must be used correctly. When you have been given the basic understanding of how to use a tool, do so wisely and professionally.

# chapter fourteen

# Do's and don'ts

It may seem like there is a lot to remember in order to perform a hypnosis session; however, once the trained hypnotist learns the procedures and remembers the rules of the court, the process becomes far less complex. The following do's and don'ts may be of some assistance with this. These lists were provided by Fran Renner and Nell Orndorf, experts in the field of hypnosis but especially forensic hypnosis. Their training facility, the Ohio Academy of Hypnosis, is located in Cuyahoga Falls. The information comes from their *Basic Forensic Hypnosis* notebook.

## *Investigative hypnosis don'ts*

1. Don't use hypnosis on any defendant, suspect, or person suspected of being involved in the crime. Remember that if a person can lie outside of hypnosis, they can lie in hypnosis so there is little benefit to using hypnosis on a suspect.
2. Don't rush the hypnosis session. Take your time. Remember that you are to provide a restful feeling so subjects can slip into hypnosis. They must have the feeling that they have all the time in the world. Refrain from asking questions too quickly, as the subject is relaxed and will respond slowly. Patience is the key to a successful hypnosis session.
3. Don't ever con, trick, or try to force someone into hypnosis. After all you have read to this point, you should know that doing so is unethical. If the subject has no confidence in you, there is no need to proceed further. Professionalism and competence will provide the hypnotist with the ability to gain the subject's willingness to participate.
4. Don't ever touch your subject, even as a deepening technique, without securing his permission first. A touch without permission can jar someone out of hypnosis or be misconstrued as an improper advance. Always have a professional purpose when you touch and always ask for permission. It only takes a word or two, which will make a great difference during the session.

5. Don't work alone; always have a witness in the room with you. If the subject is of the opposite sex, try to have a witness in the room who is of the same sex as the subject. If you cannot have a witness present, make sure each session is recorded and video taped.
6. Don't fall into the trap of believing that hypnosis is a truth serum. Keep in mind that people can and do lie or confabulate while under hypnosis. The hypnotist must keep the abilities and limitations of hypnosis in mind and not mix myths with facts.
7. Don't have the case investigator be the one who performs the hypnosis session. The case investigator has all the facts in the case and there is the possibility that he could lead the witness or victim in the direction the investigator wants him to go. A person could be implicated who in fact did not have anything to do with the crime being investigated. By having a hypnotist who is not associated with the case, objectivity is maintained and there is less chance of the subject being influenced.
8. Don't use the word "hypnotism" when talking to a subject; use the word "hypnosis" instead. This may seem like a matter of semantics, but the word "hypnosis" seems more acceptable than "hypnotism".
9. Don't ever make deals in exchange for someone agreeing to go into hypnosis. The subject must want to undergo hypnosis willingly. You must have all three elements for hypnosis to take place (confidence, willingness, and freedom from fear). Trust must be present for the hypnosis session to be successful.
10. Don't get so wrapped up with the subject and the crime that you become emotionally tied to the success or failure of the session. Remember, you are only trying to enhance the witness' memory, not magically solve the crime. The hypnotist does not solve crimes, but information gained from subjects and backed by corroborating evidence can.
11. Don't ever ask an embarrassing question of your subject. This is unprofessional and could lead to the subject putting up defenses against you. You could lose the trust necessary for a successful session. The more professional the hypnotist is, the more likely it is that the subject will place his confidence in him.
12. Don't perform any therapeutic suggestions during the forensic session, even if you are qualified to do so. The forensic setting is intended to gather information only. If the subject is inclined to return to you for treatment at a later date, that is for him to decide, but you will have to wait for the case to be resolved before you can see them on a clinical basis. It would be a conflict of interest to see a subject professionally while the case is still being investigated.
13. Don't place the subject into a deep state of hypnosis. A light stage will provide the memory refresher required to obtain details of the crime. The subject having to be in a deep trance is a common myth and one

that needs to be explained away during the interview phase of the forensic hypnosis session.

14. Don't refer to hypnosis as "sleep" or an "unconscious state" when discussing hypnosis with the subject Explain to him that he will hear everything that is said during the session, will be able to speak during the session, and will not go into a deep trance in which he will not know what he is doing or saying. Find out the subject's impression of hypnosis and help him to understand its true nature and abilities.
15. Don't use hypnosis as a game for entertainment or try to impress friends or party-goers. In law enforcement, hypnosis is an investigative tool and deserves to be treated like any other tool utilized to combat crime. The credibility of the hypnotist will be as much a part of the trial as the session itself. Proper conduct will ensure success against a defense attorney's cross-examination.
16. Don't use the word "try" when speaking about the session. Always be positive that the subject will remember the incident in more detail. The word "try" implies failure. Instead of saying "try", say "you will" or "you can". A positively phrased expression can offer encouragement and help the subconscious to overcome self-imposed limitations.
17. Don't ask a leading question during the hypnosis session. Keep your responses to verifying what the subject is seeing, hearing, smelling, touching, and, if applicable, tasting. This is one of the most important things to remember. Asking a leading question can make the entire session inadmissible in court and could ruin the potential testimony of a witness or victim in a criminal case.
18. Don't have spouses, relatives, or boy- or girlfriends present during the hypnosis session. The only exception would be allowing a parent to observe a session for the comfort of his child. Other individuals, no matter how well intentioned, can become more of a diversion during the session than a help.
19. Don't promise anyone results. Hypnosis is not a sure thing and is very dependent on the subject. Do not give the false impression to the subject or the investigator that you can solve the case through hypnosis.
20. Don't use hypnosis as a last resort in a case. It is best utilized for cases in which a witness' memory needs to be refreshed to obtain more details for the investigator. Remember, hypnosis does not solve crimes; it only helps gather new details to help investigators.
21. Don't perform hypnosis (if you are a police officer) while in uniform, and don't show such items of your trade as your firearm and handcuffs. Hypnosis is best performed while wearing civilian clothes, preferably a suit and tie. Remember, you are presenting yourself as a professional, and a proper dress code gets this message across visually. The presence of an authority figure, such as an officer in uniform, can be enough to prevent a person from relaxing.

22. Don't perform a hypnosis session on a subject just to see what he knows. Each forensic session must have a purpose, with the information desired firmly in mind. If, during the session, other details come to light those can then be explored. The session's purpose must be clear to all involved.
23. Don't forget that all the information obtained from the hypnosis session must be corroborated by evidence.
24. Don't question the subject's reaction to hypnosis and the session in general. All of us are different and we all react in a different way. If the hypnotist is judgmental of the subject, the effectiveness of any future dealings between that subject and investigator could be threatened.
25. Don't tell a subject or the investigator that the session was a failure. Neither the subject nor the hypnotist can fail. Either a subject is able to slip into hypnosis or he isn't. Even if the subject does go into hypnosis, the information retrieved may not be significant. Often people only see a small portion of an event, and their imagination fills in the details. Under hypnosis, these imagined details are often removed and you are left only with what the subject actually saw, which could be very little. The hypnotist cannot force someone to report something that he did not experience or see.

## *Investigative hypnosis do's*

1. Do use the term "hypnosis" when taking about it.
2. Do always perform forensic hypnosis with a witness present.
3. Do keep in mind that subjects can lie under hypnosis and will only reveal information they want to.
4. Do explain that all hypnosis is self-hypnosis. The hypnotist has no power over his subjects; they are in control. Tell them there is no danger from hypnosis.
5. Do inform your subjects that there is no way for them to be stuck in hypnosis. There are only three options for them: they can open their eyes when your request them to, they will fall asleep, or they will remain in hypnosis for as long as they decide they want to be.
6. Do tell your subjects that hypnosis is an everyday occurrence. Everyone does it at least twice a day, just before they go to sleep and just before they wake up (remember the scale from 1 to 10).
7. Do make sure your subjects know they will be fully aware of everything going on around them. Explain that they will not go into a deep trance and will not do or say things they will not remember.
8. Do inform subjects that your role is that of a coach. It is your job to guide them back to the crime scene to obtain as much detail about that incident as they can.

9. Do explain that hypnosis and sleep are two completely different states. Hypnosis is the state of being in a heightened state of consciousness, not a total loss of consciousness as in sleep.
10. Do remember that you need only a light trance for the forensic session to be successful.
11. Do make your subjects feel safe and secure. If they are not comfortable, they will not be able to relax and go into hypnosis.
12. Do keep in mind that hypnosis is an investigative tool, not a toy or means to impress people.
13. Do inform your subjects that they will not do anything to hurt themselves or do anything against their will during hypnosis. They are in complete control.
14. Do remember that you can only use hypnosis on children over the age of 5. Imaginative people make the best subjects; people who cannot hold the power of concentration for very long (such as young children) do not make good subjects.
15. Do check on the motivation of the subject. Make sure he is not involved in the crime and trying to hinder, rather than help, the investigation.
16. Do make sure you have your pre-interview form ready and ask all pertinent questions.
17. Do tape (audio or video or both) the entire session, from hello to goodbye. Have a pad of paper handy to jot down notes and to document time.
18. Do remember that responsibility for how the hypnosis session is performed and what occurs during the session belongs solely to the forensic hypnotist (do not take this responsibility lightly).
19. Do strive to earn and keep the subject's confidence in you. You must also keep their confidentiality. Your word is your bond to a hypnosis subject.
20. Do decline discussing hypnosis cases with the media, if you are a law enforcement officer. Allow your public information officer to do this, if your department has one. If you do talk to the media, keep in mind that they have in the past presented a rather twisted view of hypnosis. You will want to present hypnosis as the science it is, being truthful and working to dispel many of the commonly held beliefs.
21. Do remember that the subject's welfare is of the utmost importance at all times.
22. Do keep accurate records, read current journals on hypnosis, attend seminars, and always seek to improve your skills.
23. Do establish and maintain a high level of competency.
24. Do make sure that the subject and the investigating officer understand that all information obtained from the hypnosis session must be backed up by evidence to be admissible.

25. Do treat the subject under hypnosis with the utmost courtesy and respect. You are there to assist the subject and to aid in an investigation. Act like a professional.
26. Do follow proper forensic hypnosis guidelines and, if you are a law enforcement officer, work within the guidelines of your department's general orders.
27. Do make sure that all video and audio tapes from hypnosis sessions are secured in an evidence area, such as the property room at a police department. Document when tapes are destroyed and the reason for the destruction.
28. Do pose only one question at a time to your subjects, allowing them sufficient time to respond as people under hypnosis often respond slowly. Do not rush them or the session; always have plenty of time available for the session.

These items are provided as a quick guide and a memory refresher for the experienced hypnotist. The important thing to remember is that the clients/witnesses must always come first. Their well-being is the hypnotist's top priority.

*chapter fifteen*

# *Of polygraphs, artists, and such*

## *The polygraph and hypnosis*

Hypnosis is not a truth detector; as we have already discussed, a person can lie in hypnosis as well as out of hypnosis. The primary tool used by police to reveal the truth is the polygraph. There is a common misconception that hypnosis and polygraphs can be used for the same end, and many people are surprised when told that hypnosis cannot be used to make someone tell the truth.

Some people wonder, then, whether a person in hypnosis could defeat the polygraph, thereby allowing someone to lie without being detected. This is a good question and one worthy of discussion, because both subjects — hypnosis and the polygraph — are complex and require training to fully understand them.

The polygraph instrument measures the body's responses to stimuli presented by the examiner. When a person lies, his body reacts to the lie. From the time we were born, we were taught that if we did something wrong we would be punished. Our parents repeatedly drilled into us what was right and what was wrong. The result of such an upbringing is that our bodies react when we lie. The polygraph instrument is designed to record this reaction, thus letting the trained examiner know when we are not being truthful in our answers. The only times the polygraph may not be effective are when the person being tested is a true sociopath, who feels no guilt about his actions, or is a person who is not mentally able to decide right from wrong. Feelings of guilt are the key to success of the polygraph.

Think back to a time when you might have had to bend the truth about doing something wrong that you did not want to accept punishment for. Perhaps as a child you broke something in the house and were questioned about it by a parent, despite your declaration of innocence. Or, maybe you did something requiring a visit to the principal's office, where you attempted to create your own, slightly altered version of the incident. Can you remember how your body reacted at those times? Probably your heart was pounding in your chest, your hands were sweaty, and it was very difficult to slow your breathing. The reason for this reaction was because we were being untruthful, and we knew it. We physically reacted to our guilt. This reaction is what the polygraph is able to record.

Remember that in hypnosis a person is relaxed and at ease with themselves and their surroundings. Think for a moment about when you were very relaxed and beginning to slip into a daydream. Now contrast that image with how you felt when you were not being entirely truthful about something. The two feelings are inconsistent. When you are worried about something you did being detected, it is very difficult to control your thoughts to the point where you can relax. This is why hypnosis normally cannot be used to control reactions during a polygraph examination. I say "normally" because there may be exceptions to the rule. There may be some people able to do this who are not sociopaths or who are quite capable of determining right from wrong.

When reporting to a polygraph examiner to be tested, even individuals who are truthful and have nothing to fear will feel anxious. This is a normal reaction. People who are truthful, however, do not need to concern themselves with hiding the truth. They know they are going to tell the truth, and, even though they might be anxious, they have no reason to be concerned about their actions. A guilty person, on the other hand, will be inclined to look for ways to avoid having the truth detected and might seek out hypnosis as an aid. Such a person might, indeed, be able to place himself under hypnosis prior to the session and walk into the session still in a light hypnotic trance. However, as soon as the polygraph examiner begins to narrow down his questions and they start to address the subject under investigation, the person's body will still react to the guilt the person is feeling. This happens because, even though a person is relaxed and in hypnosis, his conscious mind is still aware of what is being said and done around him. When a threatening question is asked — such as "Did you remove any money from the cash register?" — the guilty person's conscious mind will respond to this threat. The "fight-or-flight" response takes over, and the person's body prepares for the worst. It is very difficult to remain completely relaxed and still be able to fight or run. In all probability, the person would be drawn out of hypnosis and all his efforts to confuse the examiner would be for nothing.

Is this true for all lies? There is no way to know for sure. In all likelihood, if the item at stake is important, then our bodies will react, and there is a slim-to-none chance of our being able to remain in hypnosis during an examination of this type. But there are all sorts of lies we tell. There are the big ones, such as lies told when a suspect is questioned by the police, and there are the little ones, which we often call "white lies" and might include telling a co-worker she looks nice when in fact we do not believe that or offering encouragement to someone whom we know will probably fail at the task at hand. By telling "white lies", we are trying to protect the other person's feelings and so we feel little to no guilt about telling the lie. This type of lie is rarely the reason for a polygraph examination. If such a lie were to be addressed by a polygraph, a person's body would react less than if he were telling a "big" lie, but there still would be a reaction. Whether or not the polygraph instrument is sensitive enough to record these types of reactions is not really the point here, because these are not the types of lies the police and the courts will be interested in.

I was present for an interesting demonstration on hypnosis and truth detection. The hypnotist placed two people into hypnosis and then offered them the suggestion that when they are not being truthful their right index finger will begin to rise up from the rest of the hand. He offered this with the added suggestion that the more they tried to resist, the more they would want to do this. He then began to ask them questions about themselves and events. Sure enough, during the questioning, the index fingers of both people began to rise up from time to time, which the hypnotist pointed out to the audience. The subjects were then brought back out of hypnosis and questioned about their untruthfulness.

How can this be? First, this session took place at a seminar for forensic hypnotists, and the people present were all hypnotists. This is an important point, because there was no real threat to the individuals who went under hypnosis. They were aware of the suggestion that their fingers would react when they were untruthful, and they accepted this suggestion because they were at a seminar and knew it was for demonstration purposes. Had they really wanted to, they very easily could have counter-suggested that they would *not* react (refer to the example of the book and the balloon). Because they had nothing to fear and the untruths being detected were not serious, they allowed their fingers to react. Would I be willing to declare a person as being truthful or untruthful based on such a technique? No, because there are too many variables in the picture. With the polygraph instrument, however, these variables are narrowed down and there is visible, detectable evidence of the subject's bodily reactions.

Another variation of hypnosis as truth detector is telling subjects that they are like George Washington and therefore are unable to tell a lie. After this suggestion has been offered, it is believed that the subject will not tell a lie, because he has been told he cannot. Such a procedure may work well in a sterile environment when there is really nothing at stake, but it is different when you attempt to use this on a suspect who is being questioned about a crime and his freedom could be taken away from him. The subject will not accept the suggestion, because he knows he needs to lie to protect himself. This is why hypnosis cannot be used to detect the truth.

The polygraph and hypnosis are both tools that can benefit law enforcement, but that is where their similarity ends. For truth detection, the polygraph is the better instrument; for witness memory enhancement, hypnosis is the better method. While the two are often associated with each other, their capabilities are quite different. Law enforcement personnel must know which tool to use when, just as is true for the use of a baton, gun, or voice command.

## Artists/composites

One of the main reasons for doing a forensic hypnosis session is to obtain more information about the suspect and, if possible, to end up with a composite or sketch of that suspect. There is much discussion about whether it is better to use an artist or a person capable of utilizing a composite kit, such as Smith & Wesson's Identi-Kit. The answer should be whichever one is available at the time of the session, because both have advantages.

The composite kits are being improved all the time. Advancements in computer technology have allowed updates and enhancements to the original kits to be made in a more timely manner, thus making the kits more practical to law enforcement. The kit operator who is familiar with all of the templates and who is patient can help a witness create a very good likeness of a suspect.

The police artist is a little more flexible than the composite-kit operator in that there are no limitations as to what is available for them to use and what they might be asked to draw. The artist starts with a blank sheet of paper and begins to fill in details as the witness describes them. The artist does not need updated templates or other software because they do not have a set pattern to follow. Also, the artist can sketch numerous things about the crime scene. For example, in a vehicular homicide case I was assisting on, a witness had observed the back of the suspect's car but did not see the license plate number. With the help of an artist, the witness described the back of the car and had the artist sketch this out, including the tail lights, bumper, back window, and other markings that helped identify the type and style of the car. The witness continued to work with the artist to come up with a side view of the car, as well. In another case, a suspect wore a Halloween mask, and the witness was able to work with the artist to sketch out the mask.

Both the artist and composite-kit operator are of benefit to the investigator, and it often comes down to which one is available at the time. A person with artistic abilities who is willing to sketch for law enforcement is a valuable resource that should be cultivated and used to the police department's advantage. A composite-kit operator requires no artistic talent, but they do undergo training in the operation of the kit.

Whichever specialist the hypnotist works with during a session, the two should meet prior to that session so that there is an understanding of what is expected from each. As I mentioned in an earlier chapter, the rapport developed with the subject can be turned over to the specialist during that part of the session that concerns their specialty. Once the sketch or composite has been completed, the rapport should be turned back over to the hypnotist.

During this initial discussion, the hypnotist and specialist should set up a signal to indicate to the other when he is expected to step in. Another option is to keep the rapport with the hypnotist and have the specialist work through him. As long as both parties understand their roles prior to the session, it should run smoothly.

The following procedure is offered to explain how a session utilizing the services of a specialist, such as an artist or composite-kit operator, could be handled. For the sake of this discussion, assume that the subject has already gone through the interview phase, description-of-the-incident phase, induction, and the deepening technique and has been directed back to the crime scene.

When the witness has said he sees the suspect, the hypnotist can then ask him to describe that person. After the witness provides a general, overall description of the suspect, the hypnotist can then ask the witness to take his time to describe the suspect from head to foot. All this is done with the witness' eyes still closed; the witness is "seeing" the incident in his memory. The initial, general description provides a frame of reference for the artist that lets him get down to work. The artist can begin to make some basic sketches, or the composite-kit operator can put a basic image together. If necessary, the hypnotist can have the witness go back over the face a couple of times to gather minute details. These will be incorporated into the specialist's work.

When the specialist has a basic picture for the subject to look at, the hypnotist tells the witness that he should hold the image of the suspect in his mind and that he should now open his eyes to look at what the specialist has drawn. The witness is then asked to compare the image in front of him with the image he is holding in his mind. I usually prompt the witness to help make the drawing look just like what he is seeing in his mind. In this manner, I keep the witness in the present and, in a sense, keep him at the crime scene. At the same time, though, the witness is comparing the two images and creating a likeness of the suspect.

These sessions take time and patience is required. Several times during the session the witness may be asked to close his eyes while the specialist goes to work making alterations. The witness is then again asked to open his eyes and to observe the changes, pointing out additional alterations that need to be made.

It is very important for the hypnotist and the specialist to resist the urge to ask leading questions at this point. Because of the intensity of these types of sessions, there is a desire to jump right in after the information, trying to develop the sketch as soon as possible. The witness, however, must be the one who initially mentions particular features of the suspect's body; he cannot be prompted to do so by the hypnotist or artist. Patience is required when trying to draw this information out of the witness. Remember that the responsibility for the session rests with the hypnotist, who must monitor what is being said.

When the composite or sketch has been completed, the session can be ended just as with any hypnosis session. Once out of hypnosis, the witness should again look at the likeness of the suspect to see if there is anything he would like to change or add. It is always best to utilize a sketch artist or Identi-Kit operator before the witness has viewed any type of line-up. The reason for this is that when the witness sees several people resembling the suspect, there is a high probability that those other images will confuse the original image held in the witness' mind. If a session is held before any such line-ups or before photographs are shown to the witness, there is a better chance that the image obtained will be a fair representation of what was seen. This is sometimes not possible, as the hypnotist may be called in to assist after the investigation has been going on for awhile and witnesses have already been shown possible suspects.

Aside from not wanting to tamper with the witness' memory, another reason the witness should undergo hypnosis before seeing photographs or line-ups is the defense attorney. One of the key arguments the defense attorney could try to use is that the witness was exposed to an image of the attorney's client prior to the hypnosis session. The witness then absorbed that image into his memory, where it supplanted the witness' memory of the *real* suspect, resulting in the attorney's client being identified as the suspect. This argument may seem absurd, but such a scenario *is* possible. If the court is not informed about hypnosis, the argument could carry some weight in decisions about the case. If hypnosis is going to be used with a witness, then it should be used in the beginning of the investigation, not as the last resort.

When choosing witnesses on whom to use hypnosis, it is suggested that the investigator start with their least best witness first. If the testimony of this witness ends up being inadmissible in court because of the hypnosis session, then the case will not be totally lost, because there are other witnesses. If the least best witness can develop a good likeness of the suspect, such a likeness can then be presented to the other witnesses for them to examine to see if it matches their image of the suspect. Other witnesses can also be asked to make alterations or additions without the aid of hypnosis, as the original sketch has been completed.

A good working relationship between a hypnotist and an artist or composite-kit operator can make a session run smoothly without words or signals, simply because each knows what the other is planning on doing next. I was able to develop such a relationship with Steve Hale of the Ohio Bureau of Criminal Identification and Investigation. I would do all the talking during the session, and Mr. Hale sketched. When he needed a point clarified, he would point to the sketch or write a brief word or two. In this way I would know the feature on which he needed to concentrate at that point. This relationship worked well because he understood hypnosis and how it needed to be performed, so he was careful about what he said during the entire session and communicated as necessary — on the paper.

The focus for the forensic hypnosis session should never be lost. Whether or not a specialist is working with the hypnotist, the goal is always to develop information that will lead to the arrest and conviction of a suspect. Developing a good likeness is one of the best ways to do this, but care must be taken to ensure that the session is held without any suggestions to the witness.

## chapter sixteen

# Preparing for trial

All of the work and all of the efforts that are part of a forensic hypnosis session will be for nothing if the session cannot be admitted into trial. Let's take a look at where you started when you picked up this book and how far you have come now. First you learned what hypnosis really was. The misconceptions that have been passed from generation to generation have been shown to be what they really are. You have seen what effect a hypnosis session may have on the body. You have delved into the investigative use of hypnosis. You understand how a session is to be conducted and why certain safeguards must be in place. Your journey has led you through a discussion of the legal battles that hypnosis has encountered, and you understand the do's and don'ts of forensic hypnosis.

All of this has prepared you for the possibility of being cross-examined on the witness stand. This preparation will be invaluable should you find yourself confronted by another person who claims to be an expert in the field of hypnosis. You will be able to back up your arguments based on scientific fact. In short, you should have a good idea of what hypnosis can and cannot do for a criminal investigation.

You must be prepared to walk into court and testify as to your hypnosis training and abilities (as I have mentioned so many times), in addition to making it clear that the responsibility for the forensic session lies solely with the hypnotist. To do this credibly, you must tend to some things before entering the courtroom.

The first one of these is to document the sessions properly. You already have the audio and video tapes of the session. You also have your notes. But, you will also need to write a report and give a copy to the case investigator. Why a report? Because the prosecutor will not watch the tapes until the trial date approaches. Even if he does watch the tapes, he may not understand what is taking place. He may not, for instance, understand what an induction is, so when you start suggesting to the subject that he is walking down a beach, the prosecutor may decide the entire session is not admissible because you offered suggestions. Your report will help anyone reviewing the case to understand the steps required to obtain the information the subject could offer. Remember that the trial may take place several months after the sessions, and a well-written report will help refresh your memory.

What should go into this report? Everything that went on during the session, but in a condensed version. Any good report tells you the who, what, when, why, and how. This goes back to basic English class. A report should be able to stand by itself; someone reading this report should discover what went on during the session and the vital information that was obtained. You do not have to include every detail about the session; for that, someone can refer to the video or listen to the audio tape. The report should make it clear to an attorney what you can and cannot testify about.

A good place to start is to provide the date and time of the session. Mention who was present (subject, witnesses, etc.), who operated the camera, and whether you used the services of a sketch artist or other specialist. Be sure to include the location of the session. This could be a detail brought up later by the defense attorney.

Next I would suggest that you indicate the time you started the hypnosis session itself. This would be after the introductions and your pre-interview form have been completed. In a brief narrative, provide the subject's description of the incident given before the hypnosis induction. This should be brief, as any attorneys will have the police report when they review the case, but it should include the main details of what the witness saw or can testify to.

Note the time you began the induction technique and what type of induction you chose. Describe the deepening technique, if you used one, and any suggestions you offered at that time, such as walking on a beach, in the woods, etc. Then describe briefly what technique you used to take the subject back in time. This narrative will help anyone viewing the tapes to understand what you were doing. Even if you are not present at a review of the evidence, it is important to present your work as being professional and ethical.

At this point you will summarize the information gleaned from the session, particularly regarding new details provided by the subject during hypnosis. Do not embellish the details in an attempt to make it look like you did something wonderful. Just accurately report what new information was obtained.

Describe the type of exit technique you used (which is usually something simple, such as a count to five), followed by a description of what the subject remembered about the event after hypnosis. This description should be brief, a paragraph or so, but should include information brought out by the hypnosis and retained after the session.

To conclude the report, record the time the session ended and include any additional comments necessary. Keep in mind, however, that whatever you include in the report will be read by everyone involved in the trial — the defense as well as the prosecution. So, you need to keep this report professional and accurate, and personal comments should not be included.

Let's take a brief look at a sample report. You can design your own form for this or modify the example given here.

**Hypnosis Report**

| | |
|---|---|
| **Date** | 00/00/00 |
| **Time session began** | 00:00 |
| **Location** | Local police department |
| **Present** | John Doe (subject)<br>Det. J. Policeman (camera operator/ investigator)<br>Ms. No Name (artist)<br>Joe Niehaus (hypnotechnician) |

The session began at 00:00 hrs. After introductions, I reviewed the pre-interview form with the subject, John Doe. Upon completion of the form, I gave a brief introduction about hypnosis to Mr. Doe. After I answered the questions Mr. Doe had about hypnosis, I asked him what happened on 00/00/00, which is when the incident occurred.

Mr. Doe related that he was standing on the street outside of Main and South Streets when he saw a man walk into a store. The man was described as being a white male in his twenties, wearing a blue jacket and blue jeans. Mr. Doe recalls hearing what sounded like a backfire and then he noticed this same man come running out of the store, heading east on South Street.

At 00:00 I started the induction session. I used a general relaxation technique and deepened the hypnosis with an escalator technique. When Mr. Doe reached the first floor of the mental escalator, I asked him to walk along a beach. I then asked Mr. Doe to go back in time mentally while he walked along the beach. When I got to 00/00/00, I had the subject turn and pass through a set of doors. When he did, I told him he would be back at Main and South Streets. I then asked him what he saw.

Mr. Doe's description of the situation was similar to what he provided earlier; however, Mr. Doe was now able to notice that the man was carrying something dark in his hand. Mr. Doe was later able to identify the object as a small firearm. He also related he noticed a red vehicle with license plate number 123ABC pass by just after he heard the backfire sound. Mr. Doe noticed this vehicle slow as it passed the man and then drive off. Mr. Doe did not see the man again after that.

I brought Mr. Doe out of hypnosis with a count of 5. When he came out, I asked him to relate the incident to me again. Mr. Doe was able to recall all of the information he had provided before the hypnosis session, as well as the new information he had provided during the session, including the man carrying the gun and the license number on the vehicle.

The session ended at 00:00.

**Report by:** Joe Niehaus, hypnotechnician

This particular incident is a make-believe situation, but it should give you a better idea of the type of information you will want to include in your own report.

As a young officer, I was once told by a senior officer that every report written in the realm of law enforcement should be written with the thought that one day the U.S. Supreme Court may read the document. As you write your report, you should keep in mind how the Supreme Court might one day regard it. You can never be too professional when it comes to drafting a report.

Report-writing is just one aspect of being prepared for court. You will also need to gather information on yourself and your credentials so you can be presented to the court as an expert witness (or at least one trained in forensic hypnosis) and thereby qualified to testify to the evidence.

A good way to have this available is to create a bio sheet, or résumé, about yourself. If the prosecutor wishes to review your qualifications, you can include this with your report on the case. You can add additional information, but your résumé should contain at least the following.

- Length of time you have been performing investigative hypnosis
- Experience in law enforcement
- Experience as an investigator
- Formal education (list any degrees)
- Hypnosis training — the schools, instructors, and any other pertinent information about your hypnosis instruction
- Number of times you have testified on hypnosis
- Articles or publications regarding hypnosis that you have to your credit
- List of courts you have been sworn in as an expert in hypnosis
- Professional organizations in the field of hypnosis of which you are a member

- Other agencies who have used you for hypnosis sessions
- Additional training you have received in hypnosis, seminars you have attended, etc.
- Number of forensic cases you have performed
- Certifications you have earned (provide organizations certifying you and their requirements for certification)

With this information readily available, you should be able to show fairly quickly that you were qualified to perform the session and can testify as to how the session was conducted.

The toughest fight may yet be ahead of you, though, even at this point. Before reading this book, what were your thoughts regarding hypnosis as it pertains to law enforcement? They were skeptical, perhaps, or maybe you thought there was no practical use for it. By this point, though, you should see the potential that hypnosis has to offer, but a prosecutor who is unfamiliar with hypnosis may have to be shown its value. The prosecutor, judge, and even other law enforcement personnel will all have those same questions and concerns that you had at the beginning of this book. Your toughest fight may be to educate those who will be taking cases that involve hypnosis to court.

Because of the past history of hypnosis, prosecutors and others may be leery of trying to put a case on trial that has hypnosis involved. They may have many misconceptions about hypnosis. Jokes will be made whenever your name is brought up. The only way to overcome this type of stigma is with education, which is where hypnosis has always had its toughest fight as far as gaining acceptance as a legitimate tool. Science is finally taking hypnosis seriously and no longer treats it like some parlor trick. The criminal justice system has not reached that point yet, though, because so many myths persist. As an ambassador for the use of hypnosis in law enforcement, you will have to take the time prior to the case going to court to explain hypnosis, demonstrate hypnosis, and essentially teach a mini-hypnosis class to those involved in the case investigation.

Once you are able to show the advantages of a properly performed, ethical hypnosis session, you can start to turn the tide of ignorance regarding this tool. Each time that concern about the use of hypnosis has been brought up in court, we have seen that the courts have decided to allow such testimony, provided the session was conducted correctly.

Here is the challenge to you. Are you going to help hypnosis gain acceptance as a tool of law enforcement, one that can help with law enforcement's most valuable evidence — a witness' memory? Or are you going to let hypnosis slip back into the Dark Ages, only to return as a form of entertainment? The future of hypnosis lies with all who are interested enough to move forward, to treat it scientifically and not mystically, to look at it as a tool to be used again and again to aid law enforcement rather than an easy way to move a plot along on a television show. Only time will tell how this tool will affect the future of law enforcement.

# *chapter seventeen*

# *Induction techniques*

Earlier in this book you were given a form of induction technique called the general relaxation technique. There are many techniques, and many books are available that offer instructions on various inductions. You should be familiar with a number of inductions, so that if you hypnotize the same subject several times the sessions will be more interesting for them. The following induction techniques are provided by Fran Renner and Nell Orndorf of the Ohio Academy of Hypnosis and were taken from the *Basic Forensic Hypnosis* class manual.

## *Sample induction techniques*

### *Eye-fixation method*

#### *Instructions*

Have the subject fixate on some point or object overhead, which should cause him to roll his eyes up in the sockets.

#### *Dialogue*

"As you stare at the object, your eyes will become tired. The natural thing to do when one's eyes are tired is to close the lids to rest them. Soon your eyelids will become heavier and heavier. When your eyes close, you will become completely relaxed. When your eyes close, just let them stay closed. That's right. Now you are becoming more and more relaxed. ..."

### *Hand-levitation technique*

#### *Instructions*

Have the subject sit comfortably in a chair with his hands resting lightly on his thighs. Instruct him that he may look at his hands, stare at an object, or close his eyes. When the subject has selected one of these options, then he should continue to do that until asked to do otherwise.

*Dialogue*

"Please pay attention to all the feelings that you become aware of in your right hand and fingers. You can feel the texture of the cloth, the warmth of your skin, and perhaps a little tingling sensation in the fingers. Your fingers may move back and forth a little bit in order to increase the feeling.

"Soon you may notice a feeling of lightness in your fingers which will spread to your hand. Soon you will be aware of and fascinated by the fact that your hand is moving up from your thigh. You can help this movement by imagining, if you wish, that a huge balloon is tied to your wrist. When the hand has moved high enough so that you feel that your arm will relax and the rest of your body is relaxed, also, the hand will drop back to your lap and your eyes will close. Let your hand move up until your muscles are all ready to relax completely."

## *Chiasson's technique*

*Instructions*

Help the subject put his hands directly in front of his face, about 12 inches from his nose, and the back of the hand toward the face with the fingers pressed together.

*Dialogue*

"You and I will look at your fingers. Soon we will see them begin to spread apart. Keep your eyes on your fingers as long as your eyes are open. Now that we see your fingers spreading, your hand will begin to approach your face. When you feel the touch of your hand on your face, usually the tip of your nose, your eyes will close if they are not already closed. Often they become so tired that they close before your hand gets to your face. Once they close, let them stay closed. When your hand touches your face you will become completely relaxed and your hand will fall to your lap and you will go deeply into restful, peaceful, hypnosis."

## *Spiegel eye roll (levitation technique)*

*Dialogue*

"Get as comfortable as possible with your arms resting on the arms of the chair or in your lap. Now look toward me. Get as comfortable as you can. As you hold your head in that position, look upward toward your eyebrows, now toward the top of your head. As you continue to look upward, close your eyelids slowly. That's right. Keep your eyelids closed and continue to hold your eyes upward. Now take a deep breath, hold it. Now exhale; let your eyes relax and let your body float. Concentrate on a feeling of floating, floating down right through the chair. There will be something pleasant and welcomed about this feeling of floating. Now, while you concentrate on this floating, I am going to concentrate on your left arm and hand. In awhile I am going to stroke the middle finger of your left hand; is that okay? Good. After I do, you will develop movement sensations in that finger. Then the movements will spread, causing your left hand to feel light and buoyant and you will let it float upward. Ready? [Stroke finger from nail to elbow.]

"First one finger and then another. As these restless movements develop, your hand becomes light and buoyant, your elbow bends, and your forearm floats into an upright position. Just let it go. This is an exercise in your imagination. Imagine your hand feels like a balloon. When you were a 7-year-old child, you had this ability to imagine. Try to recover this feeling. If necessary, help it along. That's right, all the way up.

"Now I am going to position your arm in this manner so, and let it remain in this upright position. [Gently cup the elbow with both hands and position it in a comfortable alignment on the chair arm.] In fact, it will remain in that position even after I give you the signal for your eyes to open. When your eyes are open, even when I put your hand down, it will float right back up to where it is now. You will find something pleasant and amusing about this sensation. Later, when I touch your left elbow, your usual sensation and control will return. At the count of one, your eyes will roll upward and by the count of three your eyelids will close and you will be in a relaxed trance state. One, two, and three.

"Now I am going to count backwards. At two, your eyes will again roll upward with your eyelids closed. At one, you let them open very slowly. Ready, three, two, with your eyelids closed roll up your eyes, and one, just let them open slowly." [Gently lower the arm, holding the wrist and touching the left elbow to remove post-hypnotic suggestion.]

## *Erickson technique*

### *Instructions*

Have subject sit comfortably in a chair. Point to any object suitable for eye fixation.

### *Dialogue*

"Now just look right at this. Don't move, and don't talk. Take a deep breath, let it out slowly. The only thing that's important to you is what I'm saying to you. And when next I say 'now' just close your eyes. ... Now close your eyes, and keep them closed until I ask you to open them. And as I speak to you ... your heart rate ... changes, your respiration rate ... changes, your blood pressure ... changes, your respiration rate ... changes. And I'm going to remind you of the time when you first learned how to write. Just let your mind drift back to that time. You're sitting hunched over that scratchy, brown paper with the light blue lines. You're squeezing that thick old pencil very tightly. And you begin to wonder, does the 'm' have one hump or two, or is it the 'n' that has two humps? And where do I make the line and the circle for the 'd', the 'p', and the 'b'? Is the 'w' an upside down 'm'? Is the 'e' the one that's the short loop, or is it the 'l'? Which way does the hump face for the 'b'? I know it's different from the 'd'.

"And now, just let your mind drift again, to a very pleasant and happy time in your life. It can be a scene from the present, the recent or distant past, the very distant past. It doesn't really matter when, just so it is pleasant. Just so long as it's a time when you were very, very happy and carefree, just let all the details of that scene come very clearly to you. The time of the year, who was there, what the weather was like, the temperature. Notice the colors, any sounds and smells. And now, tell me, how old are you in this scene? And what's taking place?

"Now in order to deepen the hypnosis, just count to yourself silently, slowly, and mentally from 1 to 20. And feel more and more comfortable, and deeper and deeper into hypnosis you go with each count. Go ahead. Next, I'm going to ask you to come out of the hypnosis from the neck up. Just count to yourself silently, slowly, and mentally from A to E, and on E your eyes will open, and you'll be out of the hypnosis from the neck up, but your body will remain deeply in the hypnosis. Go ahead and count from A to E. [Allow subject time for self-observation.] How does it feel to have your body in hypnosis?

"Now that you know what it feels like to be in hypnosis, close your eyes and return fully and completely into hypnosis. Now to come completely out of hypnosis, just go ahead and count once again to E, silently, mentally, and slowly. Take your time; there's no rush at all. And on E, your eyes will open and you'll be completely out of the hypnosis."

## *Dr. Flower's technique*

### *Instructions*

Have the subject sit comfortably in a chair, hands in his lap. Have him find a focal point on the wall or some other location in the room. Tell him that on the even numbers his eyes will be open and on the odd numbers his eyes will be closed.

### *Dialogue*

"I am going to count backwards from 20 to 1. As I do you will have your eyes open on the even numbers and closed on the odd. If you ever want to just close your eyes and keep them closed, you can at any time you wish. Now we start at 20. Your eyes are open, and you concentrate on your focus point. Your eyes are tired, strained, and begin to feel heavier and heavier. With each breath your relax more and more, and your eyes become more and more heavier. Each time you blink the heavier your eyes become. The more you blink the more you relax. 19, just close your eyes and feel how good it is to have them closed. How comfortable they are, how heavy they are. Each time you try to open your eyes it becomes more and more difficult, as they become heavier and heavier. They will get to the point where you really won't want to open them. It feels so good when they're closed. 18, and they are so heavy, so strained, your eyes feel oh so heavy. Each time you blink the eyes become heavier and heavier. The more you blink, the more relaxed you become. The more you relax the more you blink. Your eyes are so tired, so strained, so heavy, you just want to close them and relax. 17, and it feels so good to close your eyes and keep them closed. Each time you try to open them, they feel heavier and heavier. ..."

Keep up the same type of "patter" between the even numbers and odd until you get to 1. If the subject's eyes are still open then, just have him close them. To count him out just do a count from 1 to 5. On 5 they should feel fully alert, awake, aware, and rested as if they had a long afternoon nap.

## *Induction techniques and children*

The following techniques are also from the *Basic Forensic Hypnosis* manual but were created by Dr. Garland Fross. When using hypnosis on children, remember not to use it on a child under the age of 5, and do not talk down to them, but use words on their level. Talk *to* them, not *at* them.

### *Magic TV*

"Do you like to watch TV? Would you like to watch my magic TV? Just close your eyes. Imagine or pretend we are going to your house. We are going up the walk and into your house, into the room where your TV is. Imagine or pretend that you are going to lie down on the floor so you can look up at the TV I will turn the set on. First comes the sound, then comes the pictures. This time it's all kinds of comic figures, all mixed up together. There's Batman, Bugs Bunny, etc. Can you see them? Nod when you can. That's fine. Don't open your eyes or the characters will go away."

### *Heavy pendulum*

The ordinary plastic ball pendulum on a chain is handed to the child with his hand high in the air. With instructions to keep his eyes on the ball, suggestions are given about how heavy it is. It is so heavy that it is pulling the child's hand down. When the ball reaches his thigh it will be so heavy he will drop it. When the pendulum drops, his eyes will close and he will be fast asleep but can hear and talk to the hypnotist.

### *Pen light*

A small fountain pen-sized flashlight is raised slowly to about 20 inches above the child's eye level and is brought back down slowly. The child is told that when he sees two lights, his eyes will close and he will be fast asleep. By crossing his eyes, the child sees two lights. Because having his eyes crossed is uncomfortable, it is a relief to close his eyes.

## Summary

As I mentioned earlier in the chapter, there are many books offered on the subject of hypnosis induction techniques. If you are a hypnotist, you must practice various techniques so that you feel comfortable with them, can adapt them to your style, and can feel confident in using them. These samples are offered here only as a starting point and as examples for those who are just curious.

# *Bibliography*

# Bibliography

Anon., The court's opinion on hypnotically refreshed testimony, *Suggestion: The Journal of the Associsation to Advance Ethical Hypnosis*, 101, 35–36, 1987.

Arons, Harry, *Hypnosis in Criminal Investigations*, Power Publishers, South Orange, NJ, 1977.

Arons, Harry, *New Master Course in Hypnotism*, Borden Publishing, Alhambra, CA, 1986.

Associated Press, U.S. Supreme Court rejects speedway bomber's appeal, *Suggestion: The Journal of the Association to Advance Ethical Hypnosis*, 104, 10–11, 1987.

Associated Press, Hypnosis ban upset by court, *The Detroit News*, June 23, 1987.

Associated Press, Easing of ban on testimony by hypnosis urged, *Los Angeles Times*, February 10, 1988.

Associated Press, Judge accepts witness despite 1975 hypnosis, *New York Times*, March 30, 1988.

Associated Press, Wayne judge rules against New Buell trial, *Akron Beacon Journal*, December 31, 1988.

Associated Press, Eyeing mysteries of hypnosis in police work, *The Sun-Tattler*, April 15, 1989.

Associated Press, Woman continues fight against legal system, *Herald Journal (Indianapolis)*, November 18, 1989.

Associated Press, Ex-patient haunted by memories she says are fake, *The Cincinnati Enquirer*, November 30, 1997

Baranowski, George H., Forensic hypnosis ... to be or not to be? What saith the laws of the land?, *Suggestion: The Journal of the Association to Advance Ethical Hypnosis*, 109, 2–3 and 10–12, 1989.

Chandler, Russell and Marjorie Lee, The magnet of new age mysticism, *Columbia*, July, 6–8, 1990.

Culver, C. Leigh, *The Cognitive Interview*, via the Internet, 1994.

Epstein, Aaron, Hypnosis statements admissable, *Suggestion: The Journal of the Association to Advance Ethical Hypnosis*, 103, 21, 1987.

Ferguson, Marilyn, *The Aquarian Conspiracy*, J.P. Tarcher, 1980.

Fross, Garland H., *Handbook of Hypnotic Techniques*, Free Press Publishing, Sarasota, FL, 1988.

Howell, Marx, Profile of an investigative hypnosis interview, *Law and Order*, March, 72–75, 1989.

Kincade, Paul B., Forensic hypnosis: a second chance, *Suggestion: The Journal of the Association to Advance Ethical Hypnosis*, 108, 29–32, 1988.

Kreskin, *Kreskin's Mind Power Book*, McGraw-Hill, New York, 1977.

Lewis, Byron, and Frank Pucelik, *Magic of NLP Demystified*, Metamorphous Press, 1988.

Monaghan, Frank, Warning: doctors may be dangerous to the health of your investigation, *Police Chief*, August, 73–75, 1981.

Moshanko, Cheri and Joseph H. Grahn, *After Induction With N.L.P.*, (self-published), 1986.

Moshanko, Cheri and Joseph H. Grahn, *The Badge of Competence: The Certification Handbook* (self-published), 1986.

Niehaus, Joseph A. and Mary Sikora, *Hypnosis Unveiled*, P.P.I. Publishing, Dayton, OH, 1994.

Putnam, Bill, Some precautions regarding the use of hypnosis in criminal investigations, *Police Chief*, May, 1979.

Reiser, Martin, Hypnosis as a tool in criminal investigation, *Police Chief*, November, 63–64, 1976.

Salter, Andrew, *What Is Hypnosis?*, Farrar, Strauss & Giroux, 1941.

Segall, Martin, *The Questions They Ask About Hypnosis*, Power Publishers, South Orange, NJ, 1973.

Teitlebaum, Myron, *Hypnosis Induction Techniques*, Charles C Thomas, Springfield, IL, 1969.

# *Appendix*

# Appendix

**Hypnosis Pre-Interview**

Date ______________________ Time ______________________

Name ______________________ Age ____ Date of birth ________

Address ______________________________________________

Marital status ____________ No. of children and ages ____________

Do you have any of the following?

Asthma ____ Epilepsy ____ Arthritis ____ Allergies ____

Have you ever passed out? ____ If yes, why? ______________________

Have you ever been treated for an emotional problem? ____

Are you under a doctor's care? ____

If so, who is your doctor? ______________________________

Are you taking any medication? ____ What? ______________________

Have you ever had surgery? ____

If so, for what? ______________________________________

Have you ever been hypnotized? ____ Why? ______________________

Do you have any problem sleeping at night? ____ Waking up? ____

Do you have a fear of heights? ____ Enclosed spaces? ____

Do you wear contact lenses? ____

**Personal choices**

What do you do for relaxation? ______________________________

What is your favorite color? ______________________________

Are you right-handed? ____ or left-handed? ____

Which would you prefer to do?

1. Watch television ____ Go to a movie ____ Read a book ____
2. Walk in a garden ____ In the woods ____ On a beach ____

# *Index*

# Index